Married & Alone

Douglas Weiss, Ph.D.

MARRIED AND ALONE

Interior designed by Jamie Dodd
Cover designed by Janelle Evangelides

Printed in the United States of America
ISBN #9781881292036

Table of Contents

Introduction   5

Chapter One   It's Not Your Fault   7

Chapter Two   Experiencing Anorexia   27

Chapter Three   The Impact   47

Chapter Four   Alone   69

Chapter Five   Uncelebrated   85

Chapter Six   Sex   95

Chapter Seven   Finding Love?   103

Chapter Eight   Married to Themselves   115

Chapter Nine   Real Recovery   123

Chapter Ten   Staying   137

Chapter Eleven   Professional Counseling   155

Chapter Twelve   The Twelve Steps   165

Appendix   197

Introduction

Intimacy anorexia is the active withholding of emotional, spiritual and sexual intimacy from the spouse. If you've been married to an intimacy anorexic for any length of time, then you have had many undesired feelings. You may have felt unloved, disconnected, misunderstood, and even blamed, or criticized. To sum it all up, though you have been married, you have felt utterly alone. Married and alone. Your feelings are absolutely legitimate, and your experience is universal. Across ages, religions, and cultures, those wed to intimacy anorexics have had similar experiences.

Intimacy anorexia is no respecter of gender. It afflicts women just as it afflicts men. Intimacy anorexia, thus, may likely have affected you. You may be a man or woman in a marriage trying, for the last years or decades, to be loved, begging to be loved. Over the years, you may have felt utterly alone. Please understand though, you are not alone. The world is full of many others in relationships just like yours.

Since the book *Intimacy Anorexia: Healing the Hidden Addiction in Your Marriage* was published, I have received countless emails about individual's battles with intimacy anorexia just as I have counseled numerous couples for issues related to this same human issue. The great news is that the reality of intimacy anorexia is being acknowledged by the culture at large and by progressive clinicians. Though the phenomenon of intimacy anorexia is becoming familiar in the public, however, the story about the spouse of the intimacy anorexic has yet to be told, the personal story. And their story must be told, for they too must be given a voice so that they can be understood by family, friends and counselors.

I have committed the pages of this book to the spouse of the intimacy anorexic: the one who feels alone despite his coupledom, the one who wants to tell her story to you, the reader. No matter your level of experience with intimacy anorexia, my hope is that you hear the pain and feel the strength of heart explained and shown by those who have felt unloved for long periods of time.

My hope is that whatever reason you have for reading these pages, you will be touched by the journey of these courageous men and women no matter if your spouse has decided to take the road to recovery or has chosen his or her anorexia over you.

Chapter One

It's Not Your Fault

Say these words aloud with me: "It's not my fault." Take these words in. Really take them in. Then, take the deepest sigh of relief you've ever taken. You are not in any way responsible for the fact that your spouse chose to be an intimacy anorexic.

For as long as you can remember, you have been desperately trying to please your anorexic spouse. You have bent yourself this way and that, trying to do the impossible: evoke love from someone who does not choose to give love. You have dieted, read self-help books, hemmed and hawed. But you have gotten nowhere. Well, it is time to stop your efforts and realize that you are amazing as you are. Your spouse's choice to withhold love is not a reflection of your worthiness; it is actually not about you at all, not about your height, your weight, your income, your housekeeping skills. If it was your fault then your efforts would have led you to be loved for more than just a couple weeks after a herculean effort or huge argument.

I understand the pain and experiences you have had as a spouse of an intimacy anorexic. I see, whether you are a man or a woman, you have been blamed, ignored, untouched and disconnected from for yFears or even decades. I understand that previous attempts at counseling have failed you and at times you have felt hopeless and even as if you've gone insane.

I realize for some of you that this book may be your introduction to intimacy anorexia; it may be the first explanation you've received for your spouse's destructive behavior. For others, you have been healing for years from the wounds as the spouse of an intimacy anorexic. Either way, I feel it is important to start at the beginning and define intimacy anorexia, list its characteristics and its causes. By seeing intimacy anorexia for what it is, you will start to be able to understand it. And by understanding what intimacy anorexia is, I hope you will come to agree with me that your spouse's intimacy anorexia is not your fault. Some information in this chapter is from the book *Intimacy Anorexia: Healing the Hidden Addiction in Your Marriage* (Discovery Press, 2010).

Marriage is the only relationship that by definition demands emotional, spiritual and sexual intimacy on an exclusive, committed basis over a prolonged period of time, or as the vow goes "till death do us part." All other relationships can demand some of us, but not all. Even dating relationships can demand all three major aspects but not on a committed or prolonged basis. That's why intimacy anorexics look normal or even wonderful in the dating process and on the wedding night or a month or so later things look completely different.

Intimacy anorexia can impact other primary relationships like the children and extended family. However, it's in my professional experience that it is mostly manifested in the marital relationship.

Intimacy Anorexia: the active withholding of emotional, spiritual, and sexual intimacy from the spouse.

Now I'll explain some of the key words contained in this definition of intimacy anorexia. This can help give you a clear understanding of the definition of intimacy anorexia.

Active: The word active is by far the most controversial word in the definition of intimacy anorexia. The intimacy anorexic claims no intentionality in his behavior despite the fact that he is clearly withholding love and pushing his spouse away and has done so hundreds or even thousands of times.

As an illustration of this principle, here's a conversation with a telephone client I had just the other day. This particular client was one of those intimacy anorexics who withholds love but denies that he intends to; because he doesn't intend to withhold emotion, according to his reasoning, he is not responsible for this withholding.

I said, "Let's look at another addiction process that doesn't apply to you." He agreed. "Let's talk about an alcoholic who drank for twenty years during his marriage. He drank, spent money, became abusive verbally and physically to his wife and family, neglecting many responsibilities as a husband and father. Each time he drank, he made a choice to put the bottle in his mouth. Regardless of his family of origin, biochemistry, past abuse or neglect of his own, he chose to drink, do you agree?"

"Of course," he said.

"So the alcoholic is responsible for his behavior of drinking but you're not responsible for withholding."

"Oh, I see what you're getting at," he sheepishly admitted.

Active means there is a choice. Often the anorexic intentionally creates pain for the spouse because he or she desires to be made safe, distant or in control; this created distance results in pain for the other. Active means each act of intimacy withholding from the spouse is an act for which the anorexic is responsible. Because the intimacy anorexic is responsible though, he or she can change and begin to choose different behavior.

Withholding: Though an intimacy anorexic has the capacity for intimacy, he or she chooses to keep it from his or her spouse.

I have heard hundreds of spouses complain about how the anorexic seems to give intimacy to strangers and friends regularly. This dynamic is a real one. Ironically, the anorexic has closed his heart to his spouse while keeping it open to the world at large.

Recently, a client, referring to her emotionally anorexic husband, expressed this unbalanced dynamic of intimacy sharing, saying, "I just wanted to be treated like a stranger."

Emotions: Though we all emerge from the womb equipped with emotions, many of us were never taught how to identify our emotions and how to communicate them. This lack of parental training had led to the epidemic of adults who cannot feel maturely for they cannot understand what they are feeling. Therefore, for some emotions become scary. Anorexics choose to hide their feelings and eventually their true selves to those around them.

But still, there are those who, despite their wounds and emotional-confusion, attempt emotional intimacy, saying, even if clumsily or incompletely, to the spouse, "Here is my heart, flaws and all. I open it as much as I can, and in turn I hope to behold your heart as well." This is an act of courage and one that leads to freedom from fear and thus, to healthy relating. Recovery from intimacy anorexia involves, then, education about emotions so that the spouse can feel both safe and equipped to reveal him or herself in an act of emotional intimacy. This is the goal.

Spiritual: The spiritual part of a human being is by far the most intimate part of all. Our spirit is not only the universal place that wants to connect to God; our spirit is a place of knowing, discerning, and having intuition or a sense of things that goes beyond facts.

Sharing spirituality with one's spouse is one of the most sacred acts one can do. Regardless of the manifestation of this spirituality, when we share our spiritual side, our most intimate side, with our spouse we are sharing our authentic self more purely than we could with an expression of words.

The intimacy anorexic, though, says, "No, I'm not letting you into that sacred place" for such an act would be too emotionally risky. The intimacy anorexic who will pray with others will rarely pray with his spouse, intentionally excluding her from something so personal.

Sexual: Just as we are emotional and spiritual, we are all sexual. Sexual intimacy can be an electrifying intimate event inside a marriage when both spouses are giving and receiving within the sexual encounter.

Intimacy anorexics can either deny they are sexual or engage as little of themselves as possible in the act of sexuality. The majority of male and female anorexics aren't threatened by the act of sex; it's the giving of their hearts, of connection, during sex that is scary. The anorexic would say that, during sex, they'll give you their body, but not their soul or spirit.

This one dimensional type of sex over time can be incredibly unsatisfying for the spouse as can the dynamic where the intimacy anorexic denies sex altogether from his or her spouse. In doing so, the intimacy anorexic sends the same message he did when withholding emotional and spiritual intimacy: I will not let you in, now or ever. Your pain is your problem.

Intimacy: Intimacy is your ability to let me behold you, flaws and all. Another way to put it is this: intimacy is in-to-me-you-see. That's a clever way to make the same point. The intimacy anorexic, finding intimacy terrifying, prefers to keep flaws in hiding, prefers to be regarded as altogether good. Not surprisingly, then, the intimacy anorexic has great difficulty letting a spouse see his or her flawed self, showing no tolerance for flawedness in herself, begins to delusionally believe that she lacks flaws. This delusional belief, then, highlights the flaws in her spouse all the more. Over time, the intimacy anorexic can only see flaws in her spouse. She is the good guy and he the bad.

It is difficult to be intimate if one spouse is good and the other is bad. Intimacy means that I am loved, flaws and all, just as you are loved, flaws and all. Because I love you, I let you see me, and you let me see you for the same reason. That's intimacy, and for most intimacy anorexics, they not only say "no" to this invitation to intimacy, they say, "no way".

Now that you have a working definition of intimacy, allow me to break down the characteristics of intimacy anorexia. Most intimacy anorexic demonstrates these characteristics to varying degrees.

Busy: Being so busy you have little time for the spouse is a way of life for most intimacy anorexics. This overly busy spouse is not busy because he travels for work; instead, his busy lifestyle is a concentrated effort to remain busy— and thus distant and unavailable—right at home. To clarify though, at home avoidance can take place both inside the house and outside the house.

The intimacy anorexic's busy-ness inside the house could take the form of house cleaning or garage-tidying. It can take the form of an overt focus on the couple's child or children, usually consisting of excessive time spent with the child helping with homework or doing projects to the exclusion of the spouse. I know some anorexic couples that buy and live in fixer-uppers and they are constantly doing projects and have no time for each other.

Busy behaviors can also take the form of leisure activities like reading or surfing the web. The computer, and especially the internet, is the avoidance strategy most often employed by anorexics. Online involvements like social networking, weather-monitoring, and pornography may completely fill up the hours in which the spouses could have been interacting and relating. But the computer is not the only technological device that facilitates disconnection of spouses. The television is another culprit, allowing you to be in the same room as your spouse, even sitting right next to each other, and not relating. What I like to call the intimacy zapper, the television places both spouses in altered states, separated from each other. When the TV power is finally switched off, the spouses often feel too tired to talk. By the time they pry themselves off of the furniture it's time to go to bed.

Computer games and video games are also a way for anorexics to distract themselves from their spouses. In recent years, these games have become more and more realistic such that, in many cases, they seem more like reality then, well, reality. Therefore, saving a false world from destruction, can then become, in the intimacy anorexic's mind, often more valuable than saving a real relationship with a real spouse that is in danger of destruction.

The anorexic can also remain busy with philanthropic activities and seemingly-healthy activities like involvement in sports. The tricky thing about these kinds of activities is their easy justifiability. After all, who can fault someone who is serving homeless soup, running 10 miles with his running club, making money for the family? Who can accuse the loyal sports fan of disloyalty?

"Busy" in and of itself is not necessarily bad for a marriage. Many spouses handle mutually busy schedules while maintaining marital closeness. The marriage breaks down, however, when being busy becomes a reason that the spouse cannot give intimacy, when being busy functions as a type of avoidance.

Blame: Almost universally, intimacy anorexics are very quick to blame their spouses, being just as quick to deny any blame or responsibility in the matter at hand. As previously discussed, the intimacy anorexic cannot abide any flaw in him or herself. It follows logically then that the intimacy anorexic, being flawless, could not be to blame, at least in his or her flawed thinking.

Blaming is almost reflexive for many anorexics, it's more than who is right that is at stake. For the intimacy anorexic, emotional survival is at stake.

Withholding Love: **Each of us wants to be loved, and the intimacy anorexic is no different.** Different people crave different acts of love: from long walks in the park to love notes to intimate emotional sharing, that which will meet people's emotional needs runs the gamut. Spouses are usually very aware of the particular manifestations of love that their better halves most crave; and all but intimacy anorexics work to make those manifestations happen.

This is how I know that **the anorexic knows what type of love their spouse needs and if he or she is withholding** those behaviors intentionally. Firstly, before marriage, the **anorexic demonstrates to their future spouse that they love them in a desired way. This leads to the decision to marry.** Looking back on dating, what behaviors meant a lot to you **and when did they stop? Secondly, when the anorexic gets in trouble due to withholding in his marriage or the mar-**riage is threatened, what behaviors does he do to make up **to show that he cares? Does he all of a sudden begin the** behaviors he knows you desire? Lastly, if the anorexic's life **was dependant on this answer, could he say how his spouse** feels loved the most? If you're the intimacy anorexic, and you agree now that you know how your spouse receives **love, then why is your spouse doing without it?**

Withholding Praise: **The withholding of praise is also a sig-**nificantly recurring behavior for intimacy anorexics. To withhold praise is to not share positive qualities about your spouse and their positive impact on your life. If the anorexic had to write ten things that are amazing and positive about their spouse my bet is again, he could absolutely make a list pretty quickly. So, the anorexic doesn't withhold praise out of ignorance of his spouse's strengths.

Withholding Sex: Of all the intimacy anorexic's characteristic behaviors, withholding of sex is, by far, probably the easiest to measure and the most obvious.   Withholding sex from your spouse is more than avoiding having sex with one's partner though.   It can take the form of willfully choosing not to connect emotionally during sex.

The following guiding questions, also found in the intimacy anorexia workbook, help flesh out the picture of emotional withholding before or during sex:

During sex, does your spouse look at you or close his eyes?
Does she seem to be thinking of other things to do during sex?
Does he fantasize about others or porn during sex?
Does she communicate positively during sex?
Is she silent during sex?
Does she act as if she dreads sex?
Does she hurry you to get it over with?
Does she leave you emotionally or physically after sex?
Does she shut down when talking about sex?

Withholding Spiritually: As previously explained, intimacy anorexics might share their spiritual lives with acquaintances and friends but withhold this same material from their spouses. The anorexic might be religious to the hilt, but spiritually not authentic in the presence of his or her spouse.

I've heard countless excuses from anorexics especially from the religious (regardless of ~Faith) anorexic regarding their spirituality withholding. Excuses might go like this: I only pray by myself, sharing my prayer is not my personality, my spouse is too spiritual (or not spiritual enough) so I don't connect with him or her spiritually. Regardless of the rationalization made or given, the fact still remains that between the intimacy anorexic and his or her spouse, a spiritual connection is utterly lacking.

Feelings: This characteristic can be described as being unwilling or unable to share feelings with their spouse. Having difficulty sharing feelings is also a universal characteristic of the intimacy anorexic. As we stated earlier, addictions hinder emotional development.

If you're the spouse of an intimacy anorexic, you may have difficulty remembering a time that your husband or wife voluntarily shared feelings with you without having to write the "emotional check" for the experience. If the anorexic's image of the marriage is threatened or he or she really blows it somehow, you can expect some feelings being shared but soon fades away again within a week or two after the activating event.

The sharing of feelings is an act of authenticity that can be scary, difficult or both for the intimacy anorexic. Their unwillingness or inability to share feelings can be intentional so as to not give you love the way they know you like it. There is a time when it could legitimately be a skill deficit and in that case when he or she does the Feelings Exercise with you, you will both experience real effort and connecting. While doing the Feeling Exercise, if the anorexic is not trying to connect, but appears to be checking off a box, you will experience the "unwilling" part of this addiction to withholding.

Criticism: The tendency to dispense ungrounded criticism,

often on an ongoing basis is another characteristic of intimacy anorexia. The criticism can range from low grade **put downs of the spouse, to constant and excessive vocal** vigilance about the spouses' faults. Either way, this criticism drives a serious wedge between spouses, an intentionally-created wedge, often created so that the anorexic is able to withhold emotional or sexual love from his or her spouse. A spouse who feels constantly criticized will not want to have sex with the criticizer. And he or she will certainly not expect love when a diet of criticism is all he or she has received.

Criticism in this category need not be spoken to be felt. So many spouses have told me that their husband or wife doesn't actually speak their criticism but they can feel it constantly.

Anger/Silence: Not all intimacy anorexics use anger and/or silence as weapons, but those who do use these do so with a vengeance. These particular intimacy anorexics use anger and silence to push away, punish, or control the spouse.

Anger can show up if a spouse is trying to address an issue with an intimacy anorexic in which the anorexic's flaws are exposed. Anger can even show up if things are going too well. Anger is often accompanied by the anorexic's silence. Silence can be severe and can last for hours, days, weeks or longer. The silent punishment of the anorexic can suck the life out of his or her spouse.

Money: The characteristic of controlling or shaming the spouse about money issues is probably the least common one among intimacy anorexics. Still, this tendency most certainly exists, such shaming most often accomplished by essentially treating the spouse as a parent might treat a child: keeping the spouse ignorant of the finances, giving the spouse an allowance, forcing the spouse to ask for money, and forbidding the spouse to have a credit card or check book.

Another way that intimacy anorexics control through money is something I call controlling through abundance. This anorexic, male or female, has substantial money that he or she uses to control the spouse. The anorexic's attitude goes something like this: I buy you everything so don't complain about a lack of intimacy, love, or sex.

Shaming the spouse about money can also be a part of this intimacy anorexic characteristic. In this case it's perfectly okay for the intimacy anorexic to spend money on whatever he or she likes, but the spouse has to account for and justify every purchase and, even so, is put down for purchases, even legitimate ones.

I want to end this chapter with the four major causes of intimacy anorexia. By learning about these causes, my hope is that you will see that though sexual trauma, attachment issues, sexual addiction, and role modeling neglect may have caused the anorexia in your loved one, you have never been a cause of his or her anorexia.

Cause #1 Sexual Trauma

Sexual trauma—the ravaging, and thus, damage, of one's sexuality—is at the root of many addiction and mental disorders. No matter if sexual trauma is a one-time occurrence or a regular one, its effects are devastating. The victim of sexual trauma will, most of all, suffer great shame and great pain as a result of the abuse, a pain that must be addressed

and healed. Some victims, however, choose to close themselves off in order to, as they perceive it, keep themselves
safe. The intimacy anorexic who has been sexually trau-
matized usually chooses this very approach, the closed-off
heart remaining within into adulthood.

Victims of sexual trauma, because they were sexually objectified by their abusers, come to see themselves and others
as objects. At this point it's enough to say that when one
relates to themselves and others as objects, they become
limited in relating to people as more than just bodies but as
amalgamations of body and soul. You can see how marriage
with such a person could be difficult.

Cause #2 Attachment Issues with the Opposite Gender Parent

If you are a man, the opposite gender parent is your mother.
If you are a woman, your father is your opposite gender parent. These opposite gender relationships are relationships
in which you first and primarily experienced and formed
ideas about what the opposite sex is and should be like.

If your mother is cheerful, you might easily assume that all
women are cheerful. If your dad is often angry, you might
just as easily attribute this characteristic to all men. And so
on.

Let me share with you three manifestations of negative
cross-parenting behavior that intimacy anorexics experience and that imprint them with suspicion of the opposite
sex. These manifestations all result in the strong belief that
the opposite gender parent is not safe; all women or all
men, then, become in the mind of the person holding this
belief, not safe.

This parent might tend toward the following behaviors: inappropriate shaming, revealing the child's confidences to others, unpredictable moodiness or anger, the tendency to be drunk. Or, the parent might be mentally ill. The young soul can't predict safety at any time with this parent. The child, over a period of time, concludes that his or her heart is not safe in this relationship with their opposite gender parent. Since these wounds occur in the child's formative years, thinking that a man or a woman is not safe remains engrained in the child's mind through adolescence and into adulthood. The child grows into an adult with a locked-away heart.

The second manifestation of negative parental experience from the opposite gender parent is distance and emotional unavailability. The parent might have been home every night, might have driven you to every band practice and basketball game, between you and that parent, there was no intimacy, no relating. Instead, your relationship was characterized by your often feeling unheard, and feeling unknown by this parent. The heart of this child tries for a while to connect but ultimately concludes that this parent doesn't want to know them and concludes that keeping his or her heart staying open to this parent is not safe. Therefore, the child decides to close his or her heart to survive the neglect of this opposite gender parent; again, the individual will grow into an adult who views the opposite sex as unsafe, this time due to emotional unavailability.

The last negative behavior I see with the cross gender parent is total abandonment. Keep in mind that abandonment, as in the case of a parent's untimely death, might not be intentional. Abandonment, though, is usually intentional. This might take the form of a dad who abandons his pregnant teenage daughter, a parent who leaves his or her child's life after a divorce, a parent who cheats and then abandons the family, a parent with a mental disorder who mentally departs. Given the deep longing each child feels for attachment to his or her biological parents, living with abandonment is too painful to be endured. Therefore, again, the child can conclude that an open heart is too risky since when open, a heart is much more vulnerable to the effects of abandonment and can choose to close his or her heart. Then that child grows up with a heart closed toward the opposite sex.

Cause #3 Sexual Addiction

Sexual addiction and intimacy anorexia exist in a symbiotic relationship, a sick one. The sex addiction empowers the anorexia, and the anorexia empowers the sex addiction, sex addiction being the use of sex for self-medication or as an escape from real life. Sexual addicts are unable to break their addiction to sex and often, out of shame, hide their secret sexual worlds from their spouses. Between sexual addiction and intimacy anorexia we see the common ethos of secrecy and closed hearts.

In a journal article I wrote called Sexual Anorexia: A New Paradigm for Hyposexual Desire Disorder, I discuss that men who stated that they were sex addicts, 29% of them scored high enough to also be intimacy anorexics. The females that identified themselves as a sex addict had a 39% chance of also being an intimacy anorexic. The wife of a sex addict was also at a 39% chance of being a intimacy anorexic. So, though causality doesn't exist, based on this data, a strong connection is suggested.

If you believe that you or your spouse may be a sex addict, take this short test to start that dialogue. Below, answer "yes" or "no" to these ten questions.

1. Have you had sexual behaviors that you wish you could stop?

2. Do you feel abnormally driven by your sexual drive?

3. Have you been in relationships just for sex?

4. Has masturbation been ongoing even after marriage?

5. Has pornography continued for you even after marriage?

6. Does your sexuality seem to be dragging down your personal potential?

7. Do you find that you spend a significant amount of time online, viewing pornography or grooming others for sexual encounters?

8. Have you experienced an unwanted sexual encounter during childhood or adolescence?

9. Has monogamous sex grown to be boring?

10. Have you tried to stop some sexual behavior and failed repeatedly?

If you or a loved one answer yes to five of these questions, you (or they) may be a sex addict.

If you have identified yourself or someone else as a sex addict, it's important to know what type of sex addict you are dealing with. In my book The Final Freedom and Addicted to Adultery, I discussed the six types of sex addicts. If you believe that you or your spouse is a sex addict you can visit the website www.sexaddict.com and take the six types test.

If sex addiction is part of your current situation, seek help immediately. An intimacy anorexic who is a sex addict, male or female, cannot heal from intimacy anorexia unless the sex addiction is treated.

Cause #4 Role Modeling Neglect

Though this is the most rarely reported cause of intimacy anorexia, I have still seen it reoccur in my assessment of intimacy anorexics, so it is worth a mention.

I have heard both male and female clients state they felt they were managed more than parented by their mother and father. In other words, the child was treated in a way inconsistent with his or her dignity; the child was treated as an inconvenience, a tool.

This neglect can include a child whose parent(s) had intimacy anorexia and saw no care toward each other nor any real connectedness or closeness in the home. He or she grew up with no connection toward one or both parents and so not connecting seems normal. The parent's philosophy may have been that a child was to be seen and not heard.

For some intimacy anorexics, they have only one cause that was a major contribution on their road to the addiction of withholding. It's not uncommon for someone who is an intimacy anorexic to have more than one cause for the anorexia structure to grow in their life.

Now you have a clear definition of intimacy anorexia, its characteristics, and its causes. Hopefully, now you no longer believe that you caused your spouse's intimacy an-orexia. And because you didn't cause the issue, you can't cure it. In the next chapters, though, I hope to shed light on the effects of intimacy anorexia and steps you can take to heal regardless of your spouse's choices.

You deserve to be loved and connected to!

Chapter Two

Experiencing Anorexia

There is a significant difference between understanding intimacy anorexia on an informational level and understanding it on a personal and experiential level. A textbook understanding of alcoholism or sexual addiction is one thing, but living with an alcoholic or a sex addict is entirely different. Or, put another way, reading about a military event such as war, is a far cry from experiencing combat.

You have the real experience of intimacy anorexia being the spouse of an intimacy anorexic. You have the real scars inflicted by a spouse who repeatedly chooses to wound you through the withholding of love. You have real fears and experience real confusion.

In light of, and in honor of your scars, I want to validate your experiences in the pages to come. You are not crazy and you are not alone. Many men and women experience intimacy anorexia in the confines of their home and in their marriages.

In this chapter, you will have the opportunity to hear what spouses of intimacy anorexics have experienced. These spouses have responded to a series of questions about their first hand experiences feeling married and alone in their relationships with intimacy anorexics. Their stories will validate **your experience, encourage you, and help you to see that you are not alone.**

Here we'll discuss each characteristic of intimacy anorexia. You already know them cognitively but now we'll hold the hands and hear the hearts of those who have walked miles **and years in your shoes.**

Busy

My spouse is always thinking of some other task, one that isn't urgent but one that he suddenly decides he must complete right now. ~Faith

He traveled for work as much as possible, staying two weeks or even one month away at a time during which he had limited calling or emailing capabilities. When he wasn't traveling, he worked long hours, or hid in the garage or in front of the TV. ~Alice

Currently he holds down 3 jobs and in his main job, he is heading to work when I am getting home from mine. When he is home, he is always working on some project out in his shop, in the garage, or outside. He avoids coming into the house unless necessary. He never takes me on dates or takes time for a relaxed conversation at home.

He always has other things to do. When in the home, he spends time on his computer. ~Wendy

She would fill her days with volunteer work. She would claim that she was too busy to clean the house (so I hired a house cleaner). No matter what, there was always something more on her plate that meant that our relationship (and I) were last. ~Carl

Before kids she was busy at work or with exercising. Then she became busy with the kids. She is busy on vacation, busy on her phone, busy reading. Basically I have heard "I'm busy" my entire marriage. ~Andrew

When we first got married, my husband was traveling 100% of the time for his business and so he was only home on weekends. When I would want to spend time with him on the weekends, he would say that I was being too needy. He would say that he had other things he needed to do. Because he owned his own business, it seemed like work consumed him 24/7. However, even when he went to work for someone else, work seem to be all he did or thought about. He also was quite involved at church which took even more time away from us together. ~Raina

He worked a lot. He took on projects at rental properties rather than at home. He always wanted to entertain himself. ~Bev

He's always complaining that he is tired. He uses the excuse of his tiredness for so many problems that come up in our relationship that I have worked really hard trying to assure that he gets enough sleep. I've finally come to realize that his getting enough sleep has been more important to me than to him. That's when I stopped trying to rush him off to bed at a decent hour, or tippy toeing around the house when he's napping. Now I know that he uses sleep as a way to stay busy to create distance between us.

My husband also used talking, reading Christian fiction, and watching videos to keep himself busy so that he didn't have to be intimate with me. He can chatter on for hours while I wait for sex or a chance to share my heart or hear his. He is always sleeping or too tired to have sex, go on a date or have a deep conversation. Based on his actions, to him, videos have priority over us having sex which is crazy since he's a sex addict!

He also was very busy with the things that made him look good: teaching children's Sunday school, being Christian camp counselor, serving on a missions committee, etc. As president of the HOA (which wasn't title enough), he did gardening and maintenance of the common areas, and even installed toilets for the other residents for free. It didn't matter how much I would try to reason with him about how he didn't have to do all that for free, he still did. Now I know that he had an addiction that was driving his illogical behavior and keeping him from spending time with me: intimacy anorexia. ~Trina

For a large part of our marriage, he worked as a plumber. When he arrived home each afternoon at 4:30, he would claim that his truck was a mess and required immediate attention. He would stay out "cleaning" up his truck until 10-11 p.m. every night. I would even need to bring the children out to see him so he could kiss and hug them goodnight. Only rarely would he come inside to spend time with me or the children. ~Trish

Blame

He blames me for his making sex miserable for me. He blames me when he doesn't keep his word. He blames me for his getting angry, for his checking out and running away. ~Faith

Everything was my fault, even things that he did before we married. ~Alice

When I asked him why he left the cat out, he said things like, "Okay just pour it on. I'm a failure" followed by the question, "How much have you taken care of the cat?" He blames me for his own problems and failures, removing the blame from his own shoulders and placing it on mine. He literally can't see beyond himself and how his actions or lack thereof, affect other people. He is the center of his world. ~Wendy

My husband thought all our problems were my fault. When we argued, I felt like in my husband's mind I was the problem and not him. ~Raina

Because he is better at logical thinking, he could argue me under the bus, and so he convinced me to believe that I was the one with the problem. Because of my low self-esteem stemming from my abusive childhood, I gladly accepted the blame. He uses blame and criticism to gain and keep control over me. I spent too much on food, or why couldn't I remember how much I paid for something, we just bought the boys shoes, or oh this one is classic... "I am just checking the credit card charges to make sure there is no fraud" with a "what all did you get at _____" for good measure to drive home the point. If we were short on money I was to blame. ~Ashley

Whenever there was a disagreement, my spouse would find a way to convince me that, regardless of what he had done wrong, I was doing something worse. ~Ciara

He often blamed me for his bad relationship with our son. He blamed me for being controlling. He blamed me for not wanting to get close to him or have sex with him. ~Bev

According to him, I was to blame so many things. Every now and then he would blame me for something that was just too far over the edge, something I certainly wasn't responsible for. If I tried to reason with him, explaining how and why I was not to blame, he wouldn't acknowledge my reason. When he remained immovable, I would begin "to lose it" by throwing things and screaming so hard that my voice hurt the next day. ~Trina

In his mind, any problem in the marriage stemmed from my shortcomings or unwillingness to do things his way. I wasn't "this" or "that" enough. For example, according to him, I talked too much. In the latter years of our marriage, he repeatedly sang a song to me, "you talk too much, you never shut up."

After we were getting a divorce he blamed me for the fact that we had never had sex. He told me that he never wanted sex because I never turned him down for sex. He said if I would have told him no, his desire for sex with me would have increased. It was so pathetic. The truth is that I wanted sex a few times a week whereas he thought more than once a week was unreasonable. I left at age 29. ~Trish

Withholding Love

No affection or helping with anything ever. ~Alice

From the very start, there has been an emptiness in this "marriage." It's like he had no idea what love was or how to

*give it despite my attempts over the years to help him un-
derstand love. He uses people. He doesn't have a desire to
get to know them and certainly he won't reveal any of himself to them, even his own wife. This is a man who doesn't
bond. ~*Wendy

*I am primary driven by touch. I want to hold hands. I want
to sit on the couch and lean into each other. I want to cud-
dle. I want to watch a movie with her head on my shoulder.
However, she seemed to abhor my touch. If I even lightly
dragged my hand across her back as I walked behind her in
the kitchen she would recoil. ~*Carl

*I would often ask him if he loved me, because his behavior
didn't indicate love. He might say the words of love but his
actions said the opposite. ~*Ashley

*He didn't give me gifts or cards because according to him,
that was society's way of proclaiming love. He didn't want
to go places or do things with just me instead bringing
friends along so he wouldn't have to be alone with me. We
rarely talked because talking would lead to me asking about
how he felt about something. ~*Ciara

*He wouldn't celebrate my birthday or anniversary and if he
did buy me a gift, it would be more for him than for me.
~*Bev

*I was willing to accept love expressed in any love language,
but no love was forthcoming. I would hear him say that
buying me gifts was "soooo hard." Words of encouragement never came my way. Neither did acts of service. Any
chores he did around the house were usually motivated by
something selfish or were predictably stimulus for criticism.
If I asked for him to do something for me, the answer was*

always "no". When I asked for sex, he gave the excuse that he didn't know what I wanted sexually. I wrote him a very romantic book telling him explicitly what I wanted sexually. He disregarded it, never even opening it. My primary love languages are quality time and physical touch, but he habitually found reasons to avoid touching me or spending time with me. ~Trina

I was never so lonely in my life as when I was married to this man. We had two good days in our nearly 10 years of marriage. Two days! He withheld everything. ~Trish

Withholding Praise

He doesn't praise me and if he does praise he does so without sincerity. ~Faith

Even when I knew I looked good, he would pretend not to notice, or when others said how good meals were, he was silent. He also would not say "You're welcome" when I thanked him for things, as if doing so would somehow acknowledged that I was kind and he refused such an acknowledgement. ~Alice

He is not familiar with being praised, since as a child his ideas were condemned by his mother. "You can't do that!" she would say in response to his enthusiastic ideas. Because he can't accept praise for himself, he can't praise others. He never praised me in front of the kids or in front of other people. But he sure did tear me down in front of the kids. ~Wendy

I have been blessed with awards, accolades and opportunities that few other people have had the chance to have. I speak at a dozen events a year during which I have been

keynote speaker. I've received exclusive awards. She has acknowledged these accomplishments at times. However, largely her response is to warn me to not get too big a head about them. ~Carl

I rarely hear spontaneous praise. ~Andrew

At times he would say thank you for the meal, but he would praise me so rarely that I have to stop and really think to remember an example. He used to say I was better at public speaking than him, but even that was said with a twist of "poor me" instead of with celebration. ~Ashley

He wouldn't want me to take something the wrong way so he wouldn't bother giving any praise at all. ~Ciara

For 18 years of our married life, I did baking and cake decorating out of our home. Many times, I would create a wedding cake that took 20+ hours to make. Everyone who saw it just raved about it. When I would ask him what he what he thought, he would say, "It's a cake." When I would ask if that was all he could say, he would indignantly ask, "what do you want me to say? It's just cake. It's going to be eaten!" I was crushed. I long to be praised, encouraged, thanked. Most of the time, I feel that the only time I get praise is in bed. Then it actually makes me about half mad since I don't care what he thinks about how I "perform sexually." ~Ellen

He wouldn't praise me unless it served him to do so; He would often make jokes about me instead and never showed interest in my jobs or promotions. ~Bev

I would hear that he praised me to others, but never to my face. It seemed that he was proud of me and happy, but I never felt or heard his praise. ~Trina

I think he told me twice after I asked how I looked in our nearly ten years together. Nothing else was very positive. I actually got a real bouquet of flowers. They were for Valentine's day. Several years into our marriage I asked him why he didn't bring me flowers. He told me that he thought about bringing me flowers often but just never did. He said that his thinking about it should be enough. How lame is that?!! ~Trish

Withholding Spiritually

He shuts down and gets silent when spiritual discussions come up. ~Faith

He never prays with me. When we go to church, I feel like he is the biggest hypocrite in the world. ~Alice

We did a marriage program at church which suggested that we pray openly with each other. She flat refused to do so. When we got to the 3 Dailies exercise and she relented and started praying but the prayers were shallow. She never expressed her desire for God to reach in and heal our relationship, or marriage, or to turn our hearts to the model that He wanted. ~Carl

He can explain spiritual things, even make many great points that are great. . . but when it comes to living what he says he believes, there is a disconnect. ~Ashley

My husband and I met at church. He was a new Christian. At first, he seems excited about his Christian walk. He was willing to pray in a group and read the Bible with me, or at least listen while I read. When we got married, things began to change. He started sleeping in and skipping church. When I first discovered his porn use, I found my Bible stored in the trunk of his car with the garbage. My husband is willing to pray out loud with our small group but when he is at home he insists that the kids or I pray at the table. When it was time to tuck the kids into bed, it was MY job to say prayers. After we got help for intimacy anorexia, things changed for a couple of months. We prayed together every day. But that practice gradually faded. Now he once again refuses to pray, saying that he just doesn't know what to say when he prays. This has driven a huge wedge between us. What is most important to me seems least important to him. ~Ellen

He wouldn't talk to me about God or listen while I discussed my struggles with spirituality. Then suddenly he'd want to go to church and expect all of us to fall in line. ~Bev

He taught children's Sunday school, served as an elder at our church, worked as the game leader at AWANA, and as a camp counselor one week each summer, but he would never act as our family's spiritual leader. The only prayer he led was for the food at meals. Once in a while we would start a devotional book or study as a couple, but after a few times we would end up in such a fight that I wouldn't want to pick it up again. He has later admitted that he would pick those fights purposely to sabotage us. ~Trina

Withholding Sexuality

He controls when and where and if sex will happen. When we do have sex, he makes it lousy for me and satisfies himself only.

He never would make the first move sexually, never would be actively involved, just passively laid there and let me do everything. He never tried to please me at all and actually treated me like I was irrelevant. If I wouldn't have sex with him, he wasn't fazed because he had an awesome back up plan in his porn. ~Alice

The honeymoon was like going to a Drs. office for a gyne-cological exam. No love, no intimacy, no sharing. After that, sex continued to be mechanical and focused only on "what felt good". After years of being used like this, I asked him to sleep elsewhere. Sex with him had become repulsive. He had gotten to the point of yelling "When are we gonna do something??" ~Wendy

Sex was always at my request, in the dark, and lacking in energy. She wouldn't wear anything sexy. We never "made out". After our son was born, she really began to not want to have sex at all. We'd go weeks with no sexual contact. Eventually my frustrations would boil over and she would relent and have sex to appease me. ~Carl

Before we were married, we couldn't keep our hands off each other. However, the day we said, "I do", everything changed. It was a month and a half after our wedding, be-fore we ever had sexual intercourse. On our honeymoon, my husband seemed to have lost all interest in having any kind of sexual connection with me. At first, he said it was be-cause we were staying at a bed and breakfast for our honey-moon and he felt weird having sex in someone else's house. However, when we got home, he still wasn't interested and his excuses for not having sex changed to being afraid to have kids or being too tired or too stressed. I can probably count on my two hands how many times we have had sex in our 12 years of marriage, the last time of which was in March 2006. For a while, I often asked for sex, but I eventu-ally stopped because I was tired of being turned down. Most men would have be overjoyed to have a wife so interested in

sex, but my husband seemed to find it to be an annoyance.
~Raina

This is one characteristic of our marriage that from early on I never understood. I had heard all the talk of men being "sexual" and wanting sex often, yet it seemed to me he rarely did anything to show interest in me physically. At other times, he was forceful, demanding that I have sex with him and refusing to take no for an answer. ~Ashley

He didn't withhold physically, but because of his sexual addiction I often felt disconnected, objectified, unloved. ~Bev

The dying of our sex life began almost immediately after we got married. Sex with my husband became less and less frequent. Sometimes it hurt that we had so little sex; other times as I would anticipate sex, I felt I would really rather not have sex with him. Now I know that my reaction against sex was caused by the tricks he used to cause me to no longer enjoy sex. On my own, I have tried to achieve normal marital relations by many different means thinking that maybe this would fix our marriage, but none have worked for long. I've tried various means to see improvement in this area of our relationship, such as asking (and sometimes begging) for sex, writing letters, dressing seductively, being sexually aggressive in my speech and behavior. But still, nothing worked. At one point we went 8 years with no sex. Since then, I've given up on sex with my husband. I grieved and went on with my life. ~Trina

We had sex in the evening after our wedding. The morning after our wedding as I was cooking breakfast, I started to flirt with him to let him know I was interested in having sex again. He told me that my behavior was ridiculous. He told me that now we were married we didn't need to have sex.

I was shocked! A twenty-one year old man who didn't want to have sex? When we did have sex, it was lifeless with little attention to my pleasure. It was no fun. ~Trish

Feelings

His face was like stone. He actually made this huge effort to appear emotionless. ~Alice

You would think that after 32 years of marriage that we would know each other really well. Nothing could be further from the truth. The reality is that I don't know him any better than I did the day we met. Not any better! His heart is still completely shut off from me and he only shows emotion during the occasional anger outburst. I have felt neglected, abandoned, forgotten, belittled, dismissed, unwanted. My relationship with him is the most intensely painful thing I have ever been through. ~Wendy

She never shared her feelings. She thought if we talked about the transactions of the day and about our schedules for the next day, we were connecting. We never talked about growing old together, shared goals, or our perspectives about life. We didn't talk about her struggles with her family. I never knew when she was angry or disappointed with her sister. I'd ask how her day went and I'd get "I've got no complaints." ~Carl

Well he told someone not that long ago that for years he has been confused about the role of feelings in his life. He found my comments about feelings not being right or wrong, off base and crazy. ~Ashley

My husband lost his mother at the age of 12. He decided at that time that he wasn't going to cry at her funeral. It

seems that he shut off all feelings from that moment on. Despite a brief stint in counseling, he still hates to share his feelings. When asked how he feels about something he very often responds by saying, "BAH". The fact that I am a very emotional person compounds our problems. I desperate long to connect on an emotional level but get nothing in response. We did Dr. Doug's exercises for about 3 months till my husband decided that it just became too boring, routine, and lifeless. I wonder if my husband's choice is explained by the fact that he didn't want to feel, think, deal with anything below the surface anymore. ~Ellen

He wouldn't share feelings willingly. He would only share if we were in crisis. ~Bev

The only feelings he would ever share were some shade of anger. While he never laid a hand on me, he was very angry and violent almost all the time. ~Trina

He became absolutely uncomfortable when I would share my feelings. Sometimes, he became explosive if I shared anything that wasn't positive. He was not developed emotionally enough to understand the difference between discussing problems in a healthy way and criticizing. ~Trish

Criticism

I was successful in many areas, but he would manage to find the tiniest most insignificant things to gripe about . I was earning well over $25,000 per month in my business, and he was complaining that he never knew where to find the towels in the closet. ~Alice

I'd try to help her in the kitchen and she'd tell me I was doing it wrong. Or, she'd let me finish and then return to the

kitchen and redo what I had just done. Everything had to be her way. Criticism isn't just verbal; it can be expressed in actions as well. ~Carl

When with friends or often with my adult daughters he will make comments about something I have not done up to par, or subtle put downs. ~Ciara

When we first got married (22 years ago), I was the butt of every joke. He used to tell me that I talked too much and that I needed to get off of the phone. It actually got bad enough that my friends were afraid to call me because they knew how mad he got when they did.   It was my fault that we didn't have enough money, that we didn't have the right food, that laundry wasn't done. You name it, it was my fault, even though he was in the next room watching TV. Most of my married life I have felt that nothing I do is quite good enough. ~Ellen

He cloaks his criticisms in curiosity, disguising them as questions. A few classic questions are the "why is…", "why did you…? and the "why did you say it that way?" questions. Once I started feeling my heart, I could recognize these as criticism when they hurt. ~Trina

In a nutshell, his criticism was constant. I was devastated on a regular basis. Thank God I knew I was not innately wrong and that something was wrong with him. ~Trish

Anger/Silence

If I ever brought up anything at all in an attempt to address an issue in our relationship, he would stop talking to me for days or sometimes weeks. It was as if he was punishing me for having a voice or having the bravery to talk about what was bugging me. So then I got trained to not bring up stuff. ~Alice

He likes to motivate and control through anger. If we start to have a discussion about something, the moment our conversation dips below the surface, he will angrily say, "Okay, I'm done" and walk away. We never resolve what we're discussing. The very next day everything is fine in his world, like nothing ever happened. Therefore, nothing ever gets resolved. ~Wendy

He used silence more than outright anger. He'd often withhold information, giving me just enough to make me think that he was being honest only to find out later there was more to the story. This behavior drove me nuts. ~Ashley

If blaming me for causing the problem didn't work to shut me up, he would leave the room while I was talking. Or he would start yelling. His anger would make me feel hurt and I would retreat and be silent. ~Ciara

Honestly, we both get stuck in a pattern of becoming silent in response to problems. ~Ellen

I would beg him to engage me in an adult conversation to discuss child-rearing issues, etc but he would just stay quiet. ~Bev

My husband would go to bed in the middle of a screaming match. He'd get up in the morning before I did and when he got home, he would remain silent while trying to pretend that nothing was wrong. When he finally needed to talk to me about something, I would refuse to talk until he addressed the fight. It was amazing that he always knew just what he needed to apologize for by that time. ~Trina

When he would get angry with me, he would not speak to me for a week. As I am an extrovert, his "punishment" was especially cruel. If he wasn't silent, his anger was so intense, he would "blow up" and yell at me which was scary. Three weeks into the marriage, I asked him to sit down. When he did, I told him things weren't working and that we need to talk. He rose violently, turned around at me and flung his arms as if he were going to slap my face, missing my nose by about four inches. He yelled, "We don't need to talk! There is nothing wrong! We are fine!" Since I was a "good little Baptist girl" raised in a home where the underlying message was, "you stay together no matter how bad it is." I stayed when I should have run for my life and for the life of my unborn children. To this day because he has never hit me, he believes he was not abusive. The denial is unbelievable.
~Trish

Money

He has always controlled our money. But, not understanding the importance of boundaries and communication, he has left me ignorant. He would control 100% of our finances, (saying that I was busy with the kids and besides he's an accountant) and I would control 0%. He had to know every dime I spent. But he didn't have to tell me. ~Wendy

My husband thought I always spent too much money, though ironically, I was the one responsible for buying all the food, clothes, supplies, etc for the family so it made sense that I needed to spend money and even though I tried to be as frugal as possible, when money was tight, he always thought it was my fault. When our daughter was born and I became a stay-at-home mom, our issues with money increased. We had always said that all the money we each made belonged to both of us. Now, it seemed like my husband felt that because he was the only one making money, he should be the one to make all financial decisions which I totally didn't agree with. ~Raina

Throughout our 8 years of being married, we lived hand-to-mouth. Once we had an extra $60 dollars. I was planning when he got home from work with his paycheck to bring up a conversation about what "we" would like to do with this extra money. When he got home, he had already spent the sixty dollars for a car radio for his work truck that we did not even own. I was livid. ~Trish

Chapter Three

The Impact

Living with an intimacy anorexic is quite painful. During the past twenty or more years in my private practice I have seen countless tears streaming from the eyes of women and men married to intimacy anorexics.

The pain's intensity is different from person to person depending on how sorely the individual in question desires to be loved. No matter the level of pain, however, the impact of an intimacy anorexic on his or her spouse is always real, always searing. In this section you will witness some of this pain as it emanates from the words of the spouses of intimacy anorexics.

In my survey, I asked spouses like yourself to state in general how their marital relationships have been painful for them. Then I asked them to comment on how living with an anorexic spouse has impacted areas of their lives like self esteem and sex life.

I have provided these stories to again encourage you that you are not alone. These spouses will have experienced what you too have experienced showing the commonality and reasonableness of reactions. You are not crazy and you too can speak about your experiences.

Generally

Living with an anorexic has been very painful. The loneliness and rejection are immeasurable. The grief over love withheld by my spouse is continual.

Here is a list of the different ways I feel living with an anorexic:

I feel unconnected during sex with him (although there has been no sex in 6 months). I feel emotionally starved by him. My needs are not being met even after my defining what I need, requesting changes in his behavior, and my prompting him to follow up. I feel last on his list. I feel like I am alone in my marriage... or at the most living with a roommate. I can't make sense of the distance. Behaviors don't seem rational. I've jumped through all the hoops, but the hoops seem to be never ending and newly created minute by minute.

I feel dry inside when I'm with him. I feel like an object to him, not a wife, an object to be quickly abandoned when I express my feelings or needs. I have manifested anger from the pain of starvation and distancing. I feel the pain of the consequences—hopelessness, loneliness, feelings of being unloved—of being starved.

Conversations I start about intimacy get sabotaged or "shutdown" via walking away; forced silence; pretending to be busy; a sudden interest in television, internet, or newspaper; complaints of being "too tired". Over the years, his shut-downs have increased in intensity: from silence walk offs to multiple nights spent away from home.

Fights are provoked if sex is prescheduled. I feel like there are consequences or punishment if I share my feelings open-ly. I have been frustrated at the lack of a willing partner working hard for growth. I don't feel that I can depend on him to provide emotionally, spiritually, or physically. I don't know if I can survive if I stay in this relationship. ~Faith

It was a nightmare. I lost all of myself; I was reduced to nothing. I even became an alcoholic in response to my pain. Between the porn and his withholding, I felt like I was about to lose my mind. I came to hate myself, becoming self-abu-sive, particularly through my practice in the shower of using body scrubs until I bled. Outside of my marriage I was a suc-cessful business woman, an exc~Ellent friend, a wonderful mother. I was beautiful but I hated myself and felt reject-ed to the point of being suicidal. I was haunted in my own home by this silent polite battery of my spirit. He was bro-ken but brutal. He wouldn't hit me but he may as well have slit my throat or put daggers in my heart on a weekly basis. It was the loneliest, ugliest life turning everything beautiful black, silencing music and turning sunny days into stormy hurricanes. ~Alice

I wondered if there was something wrong with me. I won-dered: Why doesn't he pursue me? Why doesn't he cher-ish me? Why doesn't he want to get to know me? Why doesn't he want to share his heart with me? The first sign that something was wrong was my struggle with depres-sion which began soon after we were married. I hadn't re-alized that people like him existed. I was truly shocked and

wondered why he married me if he didn't even want a relationship. Over time, I realized that he just wanted someone
"around", someone to cook, clean, raise kids, and meet his
sexual needs. I have struggled to remember who I am in the
midst of all this because he is never one to reflect to me who
I am. He doesn't study me. He can't handle me sharing my
needs and emotions. He doesn't want to live in reality. He
doesn't want to know the truth. ~Wendy

I think the painful part for me began after I came to know
what intimacy anorexia is. My wife too knows what her sick-
ness is and how to cure it; she refuses to seek a cure though.
Her refusal shows that her behavior is truly intentional.
That makes living with her harder, more painful. She could
choose to be more kind and affectionate but she chooses to
remain harsh and critical. ~Andrew

Living with an anorexic spouse was very painful, so painful, that I eventually separated from my husband. That was
four years ago. To this day, he has yet to seek recovery and
so we remain separated and headed for divorce. By the
time I moved out, we had become more like roommates
than husband and wife. He wouldn't have sex with me, and
this sexual rejection was probably most painful to me. On
our honeymoon my husband first showed a lack of interest
in sex with me. As time went on, the repeated sexual rejection just got too painful and so I stopped asking. At this
point, I thought of having an affair as I so wanted a sexual
connection with someone. Thankfully, no opportunity pre-
sented itself and so I never acted on that desire. Because
my husband was so wrapped up in his work and we weren't
connecting, I worked hard to develop some deep friendships
with some other ladies which helped to fill the void, though
still, it wasn't the same. At the same time, I am so glad I
developed this support system as these ladies have been an

amazing help to me during the falling apart of my marriage.

The difference between my husband's public and private personas was also painful. In public, my husband was a fun, life of the party kind of guy and so everyone thought he was so great, but actually living with him was definitely not so great. I resented his Jeckyl and Hyde behavior. And even worse, because my husband appeared to be such a great guy, any problems I raised or discussed were assumed to originate with me. When we were dating, we seemed to be able to talk for hours. After we got married, we couldn't seem to find anything to talk about. I just couldn't ever figure out what changed when we said "I do"; he couldn't seem to come up with any explanation either. ~Raina

Relationship has always been important to me. Since I had dysfunction in my birth family, I wanted to have a good honest relationship in my marriage and with my boys. Likewise, I worked hard on my friendships, on listening and understanding others. I found I have an easy time making friends and getting to know others which highlighted all the more the fact that my relationship with my husband was failing to thrive. Why was my relationship with my husband lacking? What was wrong with me? It was an aloneness that choked me, made me feel worthless, unloved, unable to do anything quite right and yet I had friends telling me how well I did things and that I had worth. So what is truth?

Deep down, I thought that the answer was in trying harder . . . getting it right . . . being something other than what I was. BUT no matter what choices I made, what changes I incorporated, there still remained a feeling of powerlessness because no matter what I said, he had a choice to do, say, and act however he chose. When I first heard the term "married and alone" a light bulb went on in my head. I felt like someone got it. As the description of intimacy anorexia was read to me, I mentally checked off so many of the characteristics. I finally felt understood. It was true there was a problem but the problem wasn't me!!! And there was help available! But he had to want it, he had to do the work. . . and as of yet that great job of change has not been embraced fully. ~Ashley

The most painful part has been wondering what is wrong with my marriage, but not being able to discuss why I am hurt without my experience becoming even more painful. Through most of my marriage I felt alone in parenting, alone in wanting and desiring sex, alone in wanting to do things as a couple. ~Ciara

It is truly lonely and hard to explain. You don't want to bad mouth your spouse to others, because he isn't a horrible person but you so desperately want someone to know and understand just how alone you really feel. Then on the other hand, you really don't want anyone to know because you are afraid if you start talking, you will unravel and look like a total fool. So, you just stay alone, all alone...not just in marriage but largely in life, partly because you don't know how to reach out and partly because sometimes your husband blocks your attempts to reach out. Alone, so very alone, depressed and constantly struggling to be something else, that is the story of my life. ~Ellen

I can't even begin to describe how empty and unfulfilling my life has been as a result of marrying an intimacy anorexic. The deceit and withholding caused a subtle chaos in our home that drove me to become more controlling and eventually codependent. I felt crazy, lonely, hurt, joyless: my husband brought out the worse in me. I felt I was parenting my husband and would beg him to take the lead or at least be my equal partner. I would over compensate by throwing him big birthday parties; giving him thoughtful gifts; hosting his work colleagues, friends and family; giving in to sex even when I didn't want to; showering him with praise in public and at home. I certainly didn't receive the same in return. Looking back I feel conned, shocked that I allowed myself to be treated this way, and sad that we lost 18 years of our lives together because of this. ~Bev

Self Esteem

I felt worthless, below the lowest form of human scum. He treated our fish with far more care than he did me. ~Alice

I struggled during my years being married with being shy, depressed, hopeless, unmotivated. I was student body president in high school, but most people I've met since I've been married can't believe that. They don't see me as the outgoing, bold, positive leader that I once was because that person is largely gone. In many ways the life has been sucked out of me and I'm a shell of who I was because he expected me to be the relationship for both of us (Me=100% Him=0%). ~Wendy

I used to feel handsome. Now I feel unhandsome, unwanted, unwantable. ~Andrew

Only when I started recovery did I realize that I had low self esteem, and that I had struggled this way since I was a child, particularly in the area of my physical appearance—I never saw myself as beautiful. Thus, when I was dating my husband and he started saying how beautiful I was, I just ate up that attention. Even when I saw red flags in the relationship, such as his porn addiction that would resurface from time to time, I decided to stay with him. Now I realize that one of the reasons I decided to stay was my fear that I would never find anyone else who would find me beautiful. ~Raina

It was often like a swinging hammer. I would go from one side to the other, feeling good, feeling confident, and then after a season of aloneness and undermining I would sink to deep lows. His failure to share words of encouragement or praise hit me deeply. When I addressed his failure with him, his justification of "well that is just not who I am" didn't help any either. ~Ashley

I don't feel loved by my husband; however, I like myself and I feel loved by God, family and friends. ~Ciara

I never feel like anything I do is enough to evoke his appreciation. ~Ellen

Though I am still uncovering this area, I think my self esteem issues stem from his sex addiction and his anorexic behaviors. He kept making me try harder and harder with no return on my investment, fulfilling my gremlin's "promise" that "I'm not good enough," not good enough to love, to be praised, to be ~Faithful to, etc. ~Bev

I could not understand how everyone else in all the areas of my life thought I was wonderful, but listening to my husband, you'd think I was sloppy, stupid, and lazy. ~Trina

After six years of marriage, I truly felt I could not live on my own as I had become fully clinically depressed living with him. It took two years of therapy once a week and 12-step groups (1-3 meetings a week) to build myself back up. I finally realized I could live on my own because I was doing everything myself anyway. I left him after 8 years of marriage. I moved in with my parents for a time, got a job and moved *out. After a few years, I bought a car on my own.* ~Trish

Confidence

I lost my sense of identity. ~Alice

I probably "threw away my confidence" at some point. Everything I tried didn't work. Nothing would move this man to have a relationship with me. I didn't have much confidence when I re-entered the work force after raising kids. I had a fear of failure and a fear of the unknown and he had no clue how to encourage me. All he could tell me was that he never had money and he needed me to get a job. I'm still not doing what I feel called to do because of my fears, fears he actually worsened. ~Wendy

I now question my judgment as to why I stay. ~Andrew

I was expected to do things but without knowing if they were enough or appreciated. It was such a wearisome process and caused my confidence in my ability to really do things to fall apart. In public, I seemed confident but at home doubted myself greatly. ~Ashley

He didn't put me down when I tried new things; in fact he was supportive when I went back to school or got a job. Still, I often felt hurt and depressed because of the amount we fought about other things. As a result, I always felt so alone that it made it harder to be with other people, especially in situations that required conversation. ~Ciara

My confidence was nearly entirely shot. The only way I knew I still was desirable and loveable was the fact that other men would look at me and that my relationship with my children was very loving. ~Trish

Your Faith

I felt God had abandoned me. I felt that He was responsible for my pain. I felt that despite my abandonment, I was supposed to learn some virtue through my suffering. ~Alice

I'm still deeply angry with God. I don't understand why He wouldn't answer my prayers to soften her heart. To allow me in. If He could do this for Pharaoh's heart, why wouldn't he soften her heart? I know intellectually that the answer is "free will", but that doesn't make it easier. ~Carl

I have never throughout all the years comprising my walk with God doubted Him. Until now. This is the first time I am doubting that He will convict her to change further. She seems plateaued and accepts no accountability for her behavior. My doubt causes me to feel let down spiritually.

I am considering divorcing my husband, but I feel trapped by this decision: damned if I do, damned if I don't. If I choose to divorce I will feel that I let God down and simultaneously that God let me down. But I can't stay with my husband. I hate, really hate, that I feel this way and that I perceive no satisfactory way out.

For a long time I just kept myself so busy that I didn't take much time for God. Not surprisingly, I struggled in my ~Faith. However, since I have gotten into recovery, my ~Faith has grown, and I have learned to depend on God more and see myself as He sees me. I read the Bible more often and pray more often. So in a way, the intimacy anorexia and the sexual addiction ended up having a positive impact on my ~Faith as they drove me to recovery and recovery moved me toward a renewal for my ~Faith. ~Raina

I was rigid in my thinking, seeing others in a black and white manner. I didn't know it but I had placed myself in one corner—the good corner—and him in the other—the bad corner— along with anyone else who did anything I associated with my husband's anorexia such as drinking alcohol, making purchases on credit, buying big ticket items, gambling, watching "bad" movies. I was really very judgmental. ~Trina

I knew God loved me, that Jesus died for me and would have died for me if I was the only one who needed it. In that I was secure. I always want to listen to God and live in His will. I did not, however, listen to God's warning through the red flags about this man I saw while we were dating. They were all over. I was so naïve to disregard them. I felt God tell me that to be married to him would be hard, but I, foolishly, did not listen. Now I've had enough drama for three lifetimes.

A couple of years of marriage to him left me feeling very little hope. When I leaned on Christian ladies from my church for support, they would tell me, "just keep praying for him and trust God." It was so frustrating. They did not, could not, or would not understand my angst. I felt patronized. Their advice "to just pray" was infuriating. I felt I couldn't do this thoroughly and completely alone spiritually. No one "really understood" until I heard about this malady of intimacy anorexia at Celebrate Recovery late in 2010. ~Trish

Your Sexuality

My sexuality has been damaged. I feel avoided. I feel injured, like I have to be the teacher, like I have to be the one to bring up sex, ask for it, initiate it. I feel like I am in bed with an immature man who doesn't care if he makes me feel good or not. And if he fails to satisfy me with poor sex, he blames me and then shuts down. He will go months and months with no sex. If I bring up the subject of sex, he gets angry, shuts down, yells and has even gotten violent. He will never bring up the issue of sex, so I am the one that has to. When I do though, he controls the conversation by ensuring it won't happen through his avoidance behaviors of walking off or shutting down. ~Faith

I felt as though my breasts were the ugliest most repulsive things, that I was deformed and that seeing my body naked would make a man throw up. ~Alice

I think of myself as a very sexual person but need interaction with another participating person or it's hard to feel sexy. When I'm with a non-person, I tend to shut down. I used to think that his sexual behaviors were a reaction to our sexual differences by virtue of the fact that he's a man and I'm a woman. It took me years to figure that out that his issues were far deeper than just the fact that he's a man. His self-ish self-centeredness and objectification of me are troubling tendencies. I started to think of myself as an object, but I've made progress in that area. For the longest time I was a compliant doormat. I know now that God doesn't want me to allow myself to be treated that way. ~Wendy

We have sex regularly, but I can't be creative in the bed-room. Feeling wanted or pursued or sexually playful outside the bedroom are also not happening. Discussions or even mere mentions of sex are considered inappropriate. I'm frustrated because I am sexual, and like to be playful. It's another part of myself that has to shrivel up in order to re-main in this marriage. ~Andrew

I considered having an affair which is a choice I am usually completely against because I was so starved for a sexual connection with someone. During periods of separation from my spouse, I have had to use masturbation in an attempt to take care of some of my sexual needs. Masturbation helps some but it still of course leaves me feeling unfulfilled on an emotional level as I am looking for a connection with another person. ~Raina

For a long time, I craved sexual intimacy. But because sex felt disjointed and often unloving, I felt an utter lack of intimacy. ~Ashley

He is not attracted to me; instead, he is attracted to the beautiful people in porn. Sexually I don't feel loved. ~Ciara

I honestly don't know normal from abnormal! I feel so confused most of the time. I struggle to see sex as a gift from God. It has been painful more than pleasurable most of my married life. I feel like sex and sexuality have been so distorted in my marriage. ~Ellen

I was unwilling or unable to admit that he was hurting me purposely with his criticism and blame, so I wasn't able to face the truth. I wasn't able to admit that his behaviors had any effect on our marriage. The lack of sex was the one behavior that I found to be measurable. I put so much focus on his lack of sexual interest and the fact that our lack of sex was hurting our marriage that I began to subjugate and repress my own sexuality. I've been trying to find my own sex drive for the last two years, since we've been working on the intimacy anorexia recovery. ~Trina

I felt so deprived, so starving for affection. I so want to be sexually happy and fulfilled. ~Trish

Romance

There is none. I have to train him to be romantic and to ask for romance after which he does only what I specifically ask for. He does not initiate romance. I am very frustrated being the initiator and by the fact that he still does not independently remember and therefore act in response to anything I tell him I enjoy. ~Faith

I was never un~Faithful either physically or emotionally though doing so was a tempting prospect. It wouldn't have been tempting, though, if I had been in a healthy marriage. ~Wendy

My romantic side has been so suppressed for so long. I wasn't and still am not allowed to be romantic at all. No candles. No foot rubs. No touch... I have no idea how broken my sense of romance is now, but my guess is that it's very broken. ~Carl

What romance? I haven't received a spontaneous card or note or even a sincere "I love you" or romantic kiss. I used to do so much of this stuff but after two decades of no reciprocation my urge to behave romantically is also dying in me. ~Andrew

I have never been the greatest romantic but I did try with my husband when we were dating and early in our marriage. The more hurt I became by him, however, the less I tried to ask for romance. Now I have so detached from him, I am not romantic at all. ~Raina

I like romance but romance with an anorexic man is rote or robotic at best. There were and still are plenty of longings to be cared for, found attractive, pursued, and cuddled though

these desires are fewer and farther between than they were 33 years ago. 33 years of not having your desires met, you start to lose hope. ~Ashley

He says he doesn't need romance and for many years didn't want to spend time alone with me though he would tell me he loved me over the phone. It's better now because we do make dates to be with just each other, but I could still use more romanticism than is currently in my relationship with him. ~Ciara

I am deeply romantic. I love candles, little "sweet nothings" whispered in my ear, beautiful music, massages, touching, etc. I used to leave him notes around the house telling him he was handsome or telling him that I loved him complete with little hearts. I believe he liked these gestures but the fact that he did not believe he was attractive caused him to, I think, internally reject my affirmation. He was absolutely not romantic. I got so sick and tired of being ridiculed for being romantic that I eventually gave up. I was desperately lonely. ~Trish

Depression

I dropped the kids off to school and either went home to bed, or wandered aimlessly around like a ghost. I avoided my family and friends. I avoided my own life. I tried to keep up an image for the sake of the kids but I failed as I found out they felt sorry for me. ~Alice

Hopelessness is the theme of my married life. There is such a hopelessness that comes with being married to someone who doesn't want a marriage and doesn't want to do any-thing to change that lack of desire. It's like banging your head on a wall continually. Banging your head won't make

anything change, and I experienced the same failure. I couldn't convince him to change. He didn't understand why I asked him to change. My pain continues every day, never getting better. There are no answers no matter where I look, and that is just plain depressing. ~Wendy

At my core I am optimistic and am therefore resistant to depression. After years of my spouse exhibiting anorexic behaviors, I saw depression starting to creep into my life and ultimately this depression was the major factor leading to my impending divorce. I simply refuse to be depressed because I don't want to live that way; that means the my spouse and I must part ways. ~Carl

I won't let this disease take me to the point of depression. ~Andrew

There are times I have experienced depression and have even taken meds for it, but I have also taken the approach that it is better to feel the pain and process the grief than just medicate. If both can happen simultaneously, very well, but I want to get to the issue that is causing my depression and work through it. ~Ashley

For many years I was mildly depressed. I think I functioned in an almost constant state of sadness and hurt, hurt that took a long time to resolve and eventually lead to suicidal and even passively homicidal thoughts. When we first started working on the problems caused by sexual anorexia or sexual addiction I was suicidal. Then I came to wish he would die so my pain would end without me having to divorce him. ~Ciara

Depression is an enormous problem for me! My grandfather was manic depressive so I try to blame my depression

on family history, but in reality I wonder how much is due to my marriage! ~Ellen

I didn't realize at the time that I was depressed, but every Sunday night I would go to bed feeling like crying as I thought to myself, "another weekend and no sex." ~Trina

I found out later that I had become clinically depressed. ~Trish

Weight

I gained 30 lbs, lost 30 lbs, gained 30 lbs, lost 30 lbs etc. Still, I experienced the futility of my actions even as I did them: What would ever please him? What would every get him to notice me? ~Alice

I am currently obese. I turn to food when I need comfort, and more specifically when I feel lonely and empty which is a lot of the time. Every day that he didn't love me or pursue me, that he avoided me and neglected me, ate at my soul. I came up with a phrase: "Neglect is a thing that eats at my soul, causing me gradually not to feel whole." I hate feeling empty. Eating would "fill me up" and even make me almost whole. When I was dieting and losing 30 pounds, I tried to convince myself to embrace the emptiness I had hated, to learn to like being hungry. Though I tried, the desire to embrace hungriness was ultimately unattractive, so I didn't stick with it. I have too much stress and responsibility and lack of time to put the effort into maintaining a diet. ~Wendy

My weight was slowly creeping upward during our marriage – but very slowly. I reached a breaking point about a year ago, when I decided to lose all the weight I had slowly

gained. To the date, I've lost 40 pounds and hope to lose another 20. ~Carl

Years ago I realized the more anorexic she became the more I ate; plus, I ate all the wrong foods. It's like she was abandoning me by losing so much weight and so I was abandoning her by gaining so much. Once I realized this destructive dynamic I stopped my negative behavior and lost those 20 pounds I'd gained. And I've kept them off for years. ~Andrew

For years I was the same size and close to the same weight, but then it all started going crazy. I would eat for comfort or to control something or because I was avoiding or even sometimes for what felt like no reason at all, maybe just to have something to do! I have worked hard to lose weight and get in good shape, only to have my efforts ignored by my husband. Still, I didn't love myself enough to ignore him and keep the pounds off for me!! The same remains true as often the "who cares and what does it matter" sets in and I start my negative behaviors all over again. ~Ashley

I have a weight problem that may be related to my sexual problems with my husband. I wonder if I would be happier in my relationship with my husband if I would try harder to maintain my weight. ~Ciara

Ever increasing weight...goes hand in hand with depression! ~Ellen

Once he went to bed each night, there wasn't anything to occupy my attention so I turned to food. Since I've been in recovery for the effects of the intimacy anorexia, I have lost 50 lbs without dieting or really trying. ~Trina

Optimism

I started losing the light. ~Alice

It's so hard to have a positive outlook when you're around a person who causes pain. It makes for a pain-filled life. Christmas day was so hard this year because of the constant burn of agony. I knew I would have trouble handling everything during the holiday due to my living in a divorce, working full-time, raising the kids. But still everyone wanted me to host. I cried most of the day, and had a hard time handling everything. The family wants everything to work out but it's just not going to. I hate pretending it will. ~Wendy

I had lost my hope for the relationship – over and over again. I kept trying to reset the circuit breaker of my optimism with some success. In the past, I'd insist that hope (optimism) was all I had left. And now that remains true. ~Carl

I'm generally optimistic. Lately, however, I am not so optimistic that I will still be married in the future. ~Andrew

After all my years with my husband the intimacy anorexic and sexual addict, I am coming to the conclusion that he won't likely ever recover—even when he takes one or two small steps forward. I don't put much stock in his improvement as he never consistently follows through. Based on the pattern he has displayed, I know if I just wait, he will go right back to his old habits again. Because of my experiences with my husband, I think I have become cynical about men in general. Therefore, I don't hold out much hope of finding a decent man in the future although it is what I desire so much. ~Raina

I generally have a lot of optimism, but there always seems to be a choice: I can choose to believe the best, treat people well, be kind and considerate even if they don't return in kind. When I choose the opposite of these positive outlooks and behaviors, I go into a dark place, a cave of critical attitudes and "what's the point". ~Ashley

Many times I lack optimism about my marriage. I keep trying because I see change now; exercise is one of my strong coping mechanisms, one that helps point me toward optimism. ~Ciara

I was a consummate optimist when we got married, something that my now-ex-husband loved about me at the time. He loved that I would sing while doing chores around the house before we got married. After we got married, though, his behavior and constant irritation and criticism sucked the optimism right out of me! Of course, this process took a few years. I began recovery in a counselor's office nearly 23 years ago where I began to attempt to regain my optimism. I still struggle to maintain an optimistic outlook on a daily basis due to the years subjected to his behavior and constant sadness over an 8 year period. ~Trish

The impact of being married and alone are very real. If you are a spouse of an anorexic you have most likely been impacted by his or her choices to be anorexic towards you. His or her intentional choosing not to love you has hurt you **beyond words.**

The people in our survey have been brave enough to share their stories with you. As you read in future chapters I will outline strategies for your own recovery. However the first step of healing is often realizing the pain you're in sometimes through your witness of the pain expressed by those in your situation and then moving in a direction of healing. Though you have been treated with what feels like cruelty and disregard, as if you are not worth loving, remember that your worth is rich. Contrary to what you have been experiencing, you are absolutely worth loving.

Chapter Four

Alone

If I had a dollar for all of the times I have heard men and women tell me, "Dr. Weiss, I feel married and alone," I would be a very wealthy man. These lonely voices, come from the old and the young, those of different races and religions, those of different nationalities, and those of varying social economic statuses.

In this chapter I will let some of those married people who expressed their aloneness share their hearts and experiences with you. The first question I asked is "When you heard the phrase married and alone, how did that apply to you?" The second response I asked for was a description of the ways in which they felt like roommates in their marriage. Finally, I had them respond to the various ways in which many spouses of intimacy anorexics feel alone in their marriage.

Being Married and Alone

I have realized how alone I have been feeling in my marriage, like I am the only one doing the work and the only one with a desire to grow and work in issues. ~Faith

I feel so alone because in the beginning I protected him by not telling anyone about the true state of our marriage. I also hid our problems because I thought they were also a bad reflection on me. My husband didn't want me, so I felt fat (at 128 lbs) and unattractive and stupid. ~Alice

"Alone" has been the theme of my "marriage." Such contradictory terms. Many people have no concept that this dynamic exists. They have their real marriage and are ignorant of the falseness of my fake one so they assume mine must be like theirs. Their assumption, though innocent, only magnifies my loneliness. I feel I'm living a lie. Not that I didn't try. I gave my marriage my all and then some, but my efforts produced no effect whatsoever.

Divorce will be lonely too because so many won't understand and I'll be blamed because I'm the one that finally took action in response to what was already a fact: we live a divorced lifestyle. In my eyes and I think God's too, we are divorced. The marriage never took place. Did he cleave to me? No. Did he leave his parents emotionally and physically? No. Did he love me? No. Would he lay down his life for me? Of course not! ~Wendy

The emotional depth in our relationship was that of roommates. Sure we slept in the same bed but I didn't feel like she knew me like a spouse should. I didn't feel like she understood me.

I stopped telling her my deepest fears. My most precious wishes. I was tired of being told that the fears weren't real, that the dreams weren't important. ~Carl

Just today I was feeling really alone in my marriage. There really isn't a worse feeling than being alone in a marriage especially when you're trying to make the marriage work and be faithful. ~Andrew

I often felt alone even when my husband was home. There was no real connection between us. The longer we were together, the further apart we drifted emotionally. It was this lonely feeling that caused me to seek out friends and then after our daughter was born, to pour myself into her as I got so much more emotional fulfillment from her than I did from my husband. ~Raina

I rejoiced to hear a term that described how I had been and am still living. ~Ashley

The term "married and alone" totally explains how I feel so much of the time. We coexist. We love each other but it almost seems as if we don't even know each other. I feel like I matter only in as much as I make him happy. Whether I am happy and fulfilled has very little bearing in our relationship. ~Ellen

I had previously heard a woman say she was lonely in her marriage and that statement struck me at my core for it described exactly how I felt. She gave voice to my pain. When I heard about intimacy anorexia and the different components I felt validated and sane again. ~Bev

As a description of my marriage, this phrase rings true! It is the perfect description, period. I was already 22 years into my recovery before I first heard this term. I had been to numerous 12 step groups in which I heard bits and pieces of my story, but nothing rang true until I heard the terms, "intimacy anorexia" and "married and alone." After all these years, I finally felt I belonged fully and was fully understood. Thank you, Dr. Weiss!! ~Trish

Just Roommates

I feel like I am no closer to him than I am to a grocery clerk at the store. In fact the grocery clerk smiles at me more often than my husband does. My husband, in contrast, smiles and jokes more with strangers than he does with me. With me he is reserved and won't talk about personal subjects especially ones that could result in a closer connection. In bed I feel like an object or like a job to complete quickly, a task to check off his list. I feel like a pillow laying next to him. He sleeps with his back to me facing the wall and does not touch me ANYWHERE! I feel like a friend or acquaintance to do fun things with but only if I don't bring up any intimate subjects. He doesn't ask me how I feel, what I think, what I want, and what my dreams are. ~Faith

I was the babysitter, the cook, the housekeeper, the bill payer, a big income earner, the social event planner, the coverer over his lack of everything. But I was not his lover or romantic partner at all. ~Alice

He lives in the detached garage. He only comes in to use the computer or the bathroom or get food. We only discuss what I would call the "management" of the kids, not their needs or relationships or struggles or joys. He's never been my lover and he's barely a roommate. We don't share a bed as lovers do just as we don't share meals, paychecks or bank accounts as roommates would. We don't talk. We don't do fun things together. ~Wendy

She would be present but would remain unconnected to me. We would move through the house without connecting or interacting. ~Carl

I definitely have felt like we are roommates. We talk about things that need to be done around the house, errands we have to run, things that have to do with our daughter, and upcoming events/trips, but that is about it. We watched TV/ movies together. We are two separate individuals with two separate lives who happen to live in the same house and who share no real connection. ~Raina

Well, currently we do not share a bedroom, so now the likeness we share with roommates is very real. To me the status of lovers would indicate the presence of affirming words spoken and intimate care, but we don't have that either. ~Ashley

I have often felt like a roommate or even more like a parent. ~Ciara

If I say I like the sun coming in the windows, he says he likes the curtains drawn. If I like the quiet, he likes the music on. If I don't care that we lock the doors when we leave the house, he insists they be locked. If I insist that the dishes be done after each meal, he insists that my request is over the top. If I am satisfied with a video at home for a date, he insists that we must go to the theater. If I want to try a new restaurant, he only wants to go to the one we always go to. How in the world did we ever end up married if we don't have any common likes? I pay my bills and he pays his. I do my laundry and he does his laundry. I do my chores and he does his, but we never do anything together. We are perfect roommates, so why are we even married? I got married to do more things together, including sex, not this. ~Trina

I believe one would treat a roommate better than I was treated. I felt more like a maid. ~Trish

Emotionally Alone

I share my emotions with people outside of my home; I discuss my emotions with my counselor. If I get emotional in front of my anorexic husband, he disallows the emotion, devalues it, denies its validity. I receive no empathy no listening ear. Instead, my husband reacts to my emotion with anger; often he leaves the house in response to my expressions of emotion, which makes me even more alone. ~Faith He would minimize my feelings. ~Alice

I can't even describe how much of a shock this emotional loneliness was to me as a naive bride. Now that I have matured some, I would describe this same reality as an appalling outrage. To be in what should be something God created for the purpose of dispelling loneliness and have it be the ultimate in loneliness. To be in a "relationship" that should be the epitome of love and have it be void of love. I am distraught living this way. It's awful. I remember giving birth to the last 2 kids at home and the midwife leaving me and my husband alone for a time, and of course he had nothing to say. It should've been a wonderful, close time of bonding and rejoicing together and sharing our love for each other, but it was nothing of the sort. So I felt despair along with the joy of a baby being born. I don't think he even noticed. ~Wendy

I found friends with whom I could share my feelings in order to fill the void in my life, the void that my marriage was supposed to fill but didn't. ~Carl

Because of the conditioning I received from my marriage, I feel like I can't share my real feelings or needs without some type of retribution or blame. I don't feel heard anymore. ~Andrew

After we married, I felt like my husband and I hardly connected emotionally such that I was much more interested in talking about my thoughts and feelings with friends rather than my husband. And I felt like my husband held back his thoughts and feelings from me most of the time too. Mostly, all we did together was hang out with friends or watch TV/movies together—that was it. ~Raina

Oh this one is the big one. When he flat lines and offers no comments, no affirmation or validation of things, it feels like a death, a total shut down. I wonder why I should bother to share anything with him if I can expect no depth of conversation. I don't want to know what the weather is or how the taxes are going up if he can't relate to me on a deeper level, an emotional level. He is ok with being "with me" while we remain unconnected. I can do that for a time, but to not care about what someone is thinking, dreaming or working on ultimately feels like death. I have said that if I am going to be emotionally alone, I would rather be completely alone so that I can at least free myself of the conflict of being in someone's presence without having his attention. I can be alone and not talk to anyone for a long period, but if I am in a group or with one other person and there is no deep level of understanding and sharing to even a small degree, I feel like I am in prison. ~Ashley

Sharing thoughts or feelings or even the events of his day

with me are things that he isn't interested in. I get excited about sharing things with him, but sharing with me often seems to be an afterthought for him, so much so that he will forget to tell me things about our families. I often feel like he puts everyone else before me. ~Ciara

I felt like I was married to a teenager who was unable to meet my emotional needs; He'd never ask me about my life as a step-mother or show interest in my work or other accomplishments. He would shut down if I got too close. ~Bev

Spiritually Alone

I am without a partner to pray with or talk about things with. ~Alice

I can't share my relationship with God with her. Instead, I've had to turn to friends to share my praises and struggles. ~Carl

After the first years of our marriage, if I was going to read the Bible and pray, it was by myself. We didn't talk about our ~Faith much. I used the fact that he felt intimidated by my ~Faith (as I had always been a Christian and have never rebelled and I knew so much more about the Bible than he did) to explain his refusal to discuss ~Faith with me. As time went on, he even began to question whether he believed in God at all which really worried me even more as I had never bargained for having an unbelieving spouse. ~Raina

I find others with whom I can share if he doesn't want to share. The problem, though, is that I don't want to go to church anymore, I don't want to pretend that I have a "good marriage" or that we are "ok". I would rather use that time to read, study, pray totally alone than to go through the motions of being with others while I know I will only feel really alone inside. ~Ashley

I always had to pray by myself, work alone to find a church home, read the Bible on my own; when I tried to talk to him about how I wanted his participation and input, he would judge me for not being spiritually mature enough to make my own spiritual decisions. ~Bev

Alone at Home

When I show emotion or bring up sex, my husband gets angry, refuses to talk, and will often get up and leave. He can't handle the times when I say "I feel hurt" or "I feel alone", or "I need xyz" or "I don't feel good when you...",etc. He can't handle any requests that would force him to be empathetic or listen or be engaged. I am home alone a lot as when my husband flees, he remains gone for hours at a time. He hides in his car or at McDonalds. And when he is home, he hides away, in the basement, TV room or in front of the computer. ~Faith

He wouldn't help out with anything at home and he avoided actually even being there. ~Alice

I am the only adult at home in the evenings because he "conveniently" works from 3pm to all hours of the night and never comes home at a regular time. But I don't allow myself to worry about that anymore. So I am the parent at home, bearing the entire load myself. This is a very lonely time. It should be a time of mutual support between husband and wife but he works that shift so he doesn't have to deal with his family. Even though counselors have told him that even a good marriage would struggle with that schedule (I work days, he works nights) he refuses to do anything about it. He

*is fine with it. He likes things to stay the same even if they
are horrible. (It's not horrible for him, just me).* ~Wendy

*We would never really talk. We had a set time – 10PM to
get together every night but we never did really talk.* ~Carl

*Watching her on the computer, her phone, the paper, I feel
utterly alone many a night. She wonders why I take my time
coming home.* ~Andrew

*My husband was traveling 100% most of the first couple
years of our marriage. So literally, I was home alone a lot
of the time. I missed him greatly when he was gone and
couldn't wait to see him on the weekends. However, when
he came home, he would say he had to work or he would
want to spend time with people other than me and when I
got upset, he said I was being too needy.* ~Raina

*I was left to manage the household; he would "help" but
not take on any responsibility; he would commit to certain
house projects and then not do them.* ~Bev

Alone in Parenting

*My husband traveled a lot. He let me raise the kids com-
pletely and gave no input. He just wanted to make money,
so he spent most of his time at work; when he was home,
he remained disengaged in the kids' play and conversations.
He didn't care that I was raising the kids alone because he
said that I was good at parenting.* ~Faith

*He was so immature and ill equipped. He was a child him-
self, so the children had no respect for him at all.* ~Alice

I am the only one who parents. I encourage, teach, train,

counsel, provide, chauffeur. I pray with them and take them to church. I feel like a single mom, although technically I know I'm married, not single. ~Wendy

My husband and I have been separated since my daughter was 2 and she is now 6 so I have basically been a single parent. Even in those first two years, I did almost all of the caring for our daughter as a stay-a-home mom. If I would leave even for 10 minutes to run an errand, when I got home, my husband was often on the computer while our baby daughter was playing on the floor nearby. When my husband would come home from work, he would play with our daughter for a little while but often would then soon be off doing something else. ~Raina

It felt like I raised our kids alone. Yes, he was there and he had conversations with the boys, gave them many great insights and such, but emotionally it was all up to me, even physically as I think about it. Getting them in and out of school projects, events and handling most discipline was all my job. ~Ashley

He felt like another child I needed to parent; he didn't contribute to the disciplining of the children; he would agree to a strategy and then not follow it through. ~Bev

Untouched

I feel untouched. Like a dog that has been left in a pen for hours without contact. My body will go for days and months with no touch. Sometimes I get a hug or a quick kiss, but it feels mechanical and forced. ~Faith

He wouldn't touch me at all. I felt more deprived than a dog would be; at least a dog would get a belly rub! ~Alice

I crave attention and being held. He could never just hold me. Instead, our physical contact always had to involve sex because of the fact that he viewed me as an object meant to meet his sexual needs. ~Wendy

We didn't touch so I'd make sure to find people to shake hands with and hug on a nearly daily basis. I felt more touched while away at a conference then when at home. ~Carl

I have to ask to be touched. She'll initiate touch only if she thinks I am mad at her. ~Andrew

Unspoken to

He does bring up our problems so we can discuss them and never owns up to his part in our problems. He refuses to come up with solutions. He defends his actions, blames me, and sweeps the issues under the carpet. When he refuses to, I offer solutions and get called "controlling" as a result after which he shuts down, refusing to honor any solutions I bring up. ~Faith

Literally he would use as few words as possible in conversation or refuse conversation altogether using email as a substitute. He talked to his assistant more than he did to me. ~Alice

How I cherish my times talking with my girl friends! They speak to me and know me. But they can't take the place of a spouse. But he doesn't want to communicate deeply with me and that is hard to accept. ~Wendy

He only talked about work—his only area of confidence. ~Bev

The constant, "silent treatment" was quite painful. ~Trish

Unheard

*I can say the same sentence 20 times in a row and he can
NEVER repeat back what I said, claiming that he didn't hear
me. In reality he is not listening to me.   I don't feel heard,
listened to. It's as if I don't exist. ~Faith*

He would misinterpret or diminish what I would say. ~Alice

*He can't discuss anything without making it all about him.
So, when I talk about my own needs, he never really hears
me. If I communicate a need, he only hears that he messed
up, that he failed. If I communicate how to do something in
a different way, he only hears that I think he's doing it all
wrong. He can't get beyond himself. ~Wendy*

*I didn't feel like my desires were heard. My desires weren't
worthy of consideration. ~Carl*

*He didn't listen fully so he didn't hear. Therefore I was un-
heard and alone. ~Ashley*

*Basically, in his mind understanding and listening were my
jobs and mine alone. He stated that I was illogical. He actually told me once that if I would only listen to him and how
he logically thought through each step, that I would change
my mind because it made sense. Therefore, I was not "allowed" to have my own opinions. Luckily, I had about two
years of counseling under my belt and knew how ridiculous
it was for him not to "allow me" my own opinion. It was
about that time I asked him to move out. ~Trish*

Unknown and Alone

My husband doesn't get to know me. He doesn't ask questions about who I am, what I believe, etc. He doesn't not share his opinions, take a stand, share his ideas. ~Faith

He couldn't care less about who I was and what I wanted. ~Alice

He doesn't know me and doesn't want to just as he doesn't know himself and doesn't want to. Since I can't share myself with him and he cannot share himself with me, we basically aren't married. ~Wendy

I can't talk about my dreams or ideas for the future. Whatever motivates me she find uninteresting. ~Andrew

I don't think my husband really ever knew me. He had kind of pigeon-holed me into who I used to be or who he thought I was and even when I changed, he wouldn't recognize my change. Now that I have been through recovery and have drastically changed, he really doesn't know me at all and really doesn't try to. ~Raina

He may know me intellectually, but he certainly doesn't know me with his heart. He cannot hear the fullness of what I am sharing and respond to it, enter into it. How tragic and sad is that after 33 years? ~Ashley

I honestly feel like my husband has no desire to really know me. He only wants to know what he needs to know for his own well being. I long to be known! I long for him to ask me about me. ~Ellen

Your aloneness is real. Your story, if you are a spouse of an intimacy anorexic, probably is full of this feeling of being alone. Nevertheless, you absolutely deserve to be connected to, explored, and celebrated. You are an amazing person whose worth is not to be dictated by an anorexic's poor choices.

As you journey on this road to recovery, my hope is that you will find your amazing self again. When you become loveable regardless of your spouse's choices your future can once again become bright.

Chapter Five

Uncelebrated

One of the things all of us on some level expect from a marriage and from a spouse is that he or she will celebrate us. Why would you marry someone you don't feel like celebrating, someone you are not proud of? I have heard spouses of intimacy anorexics ask this question time and time again. Of course, for this question, there is no sane answer.

However, as spouses, men and women have consistently communicated that they have remained uncelebrated by their anorexic spouses. They report how this lack of being celebrated has impacted them, especially on big days like holidays and birthdays.

Here you will read feedback from spouses as they share how they have been uncelebrated. Their stories may sound familiar to you and hopefully again validate the truth that these behaviors are behaviors of anorexics and in no way real reflections of the uncelebrated spouse's worth.

Generally

No birthday card or gift for my 40th birthday; plus I planned my own birthday celebration. In contrast, I planned gifts and a big party for his 40th. ~Alice

Sometimes I would imagine being celebrated in a big way when I turned 50 or 40 but I knew that was an impossibility with him so I just gave up hoping for and dreaming about this kind of affirmation. ~Wendy

One of my good friends told me, "You deserve to be loved." I never felt that way with my wife. ~Carl

I am uncelebrated. I have to buy all my Christmas and birthday gifts or I would receive none. This is really painful. ~Andrew

Celebrated? Are you kidding? That would require his going outside of himself and thinking about what it would be like to give to another. ~Ashley

I never feel like he is proud of me. When the world seems to celebrate me it is almost as if he is angry because they are noticing me and I am not noticing him. ~Ellen

My birthdays came and went with little or no effort on his part. And forget appropriate gifts for holidays like Valentine's Day! One year, he bought me a nail gun for himself as my Valentine's Day gift. We don't celebrate anniversaries typically and the one we did celebrate ended up being a horrible date—He was distant and cold. ~Bev

His birthday was October 4th, and mine followed exactly four weeks later on November 1st. In my family, birthdays

were a big deal, so I would always make his birthday special with a cake, ice cream, a present when we had the money, and some friends invited over. He would do absolutely nothing for mine, saying we had no money for such things.

After mentioning year after year how special a Mothers' Day gift makes me feel, he asked the lady at the jewelry counter to pick something out and it was beautiful. One time in 8 years he actually listened to me!! I was so happy that day. ~Trish

Holidays

He would wait until the very end of the day on Mother's Day to give a card or gift. Often, he would claim he forgot to buy a gift. He would be too tired for sex. ~Alice

It was our 25th wedding anniversary. We went to his parent's house for a dinner and he was already drunk when he arrived. It was so embarrassing. ~Wendy

She would not commit to 5 minutes of time alone with me while we were with her family. It ultimately would send me off the deep end to the point where I'd threaten that we would be headed home early because I just couldn't stand to be present while she was pretending to her family that everything between she and I was OK and at the same time actively making it difficult to connect with me. ~Carl

He does not like holidays. I think they must have not been good when he was a child or something. He has never been able to tell me why, but he is often moody and difficult to get along with at holidays. Thanksgiving was the worst for a while. All he could ever say was that his ex-fiancé broke up with him one Thanksgiving and for some reason years later, *he would just be terrible to be with on that day. I remember when we were dating, we had some wonderful Valentine's Days, but after we were married, we seemed to have terrible fights around that time. The Christmas after he lost his job, I was very upset about not being able to buy gifts as we had no money since shopping for the perfect gift for everyone was my favorite part of Christmas. My dad gave me $100 to spend on gifts for everyone. I was able to get awesome deals and buy for everyone including something for him even though we had said we were not going to get anything for each other. To even try to get him something was a huge step for me as I was still quite angry with him. When I tried to give him the gift on Christmas, he refused to open it. I was very hurt and went upstairs to cry, but I decided that I loved Christmas and I was not going to let him ruin my Christmas. So we went to my aunt's as is our tradition and he was moody with me but sociable with everyone else. We didn't speak on the way home and went to bed as soon as we got to my parents. We ended up fighting about it the next day and he almost left my parents and went back to Ohio early. He just couldn't see how he was wrong and claimed that I had been trying to embarrass him by giving him a gift when I knew well that he would not be able to give me one in return. He thought it was all my fault.* ~Raina*

He gets stressed easily around major holidays and will start yelling which makes me and others uncomfortable. ~Ciara*

He would fall asleep on the night we had planned to pack our kids' presents. He would tell me I had to be on a strict budget for presents and then come home with gifts for the kids after I was done with all the shopping and wrapping. He bought me gifts that he seemed to not have thought out. He did not want to read a Christmas story with the kids. ~Bev*

Anniversary

He avoided making plans to celebrate our anniversary which made me feel guilty about the money such a celebration would have cost and sad because he was acting so cheap. ~Alice

I don't have special memories surrounding our anniversary. We never took a fun trip. We didn't even go out to dinner on our anniversary, much less at other times. Going on a date with him meant disappointment and boredom. He didn't show up emotionally. I'd be talking with myself. I'd rather not go on dates with him as a result. ~Wendy

Our 15th anniversary was during a trip east. She didn't even want to have sex on our anniversary. Ultimately she relented but it was cold, mechanical, and unloving. ~Carl

Many times he forgot our anniversary or he was too busy to even pick out a card. ~Ciara

He wouldn't plan anything; In 2009 I made arrangements for us to go for dinner and then he said he was sick and wouldn't go. ~Bev

I believe he did get me cards but he only signed his name to at the bottom. No personal note whatsoever was included. So touching-not!! ~Trish

Your Birthday

I get great gifts, but they are unwrapped. The card is signed but the envelope does not have my name on it. ~Faith

Minimal effort is put forth, obviously begrudgingly. ~Alice

She never forgot them – but I can't remember her making it a time for us to be connected. ~Carl

My friends always seemed to make up for his neglect but it doesn't take away the sting. The day was like any other day with maybe a "happy birthday" and a card. ~Ashley

My birthday was usually a burden because is falls very close to Christmas. ~Ciara

For my 30th birthday, he planned nothing not even with my family and proceeded to announce that he had overdrawn our Visa without telling me. He put us into significant financial difficulty. ~Bev

If he did get me a present, it was of little value and absolutely absent of meaning. ~Trish

He promises me sex on my birthday, then starts a fight so he can blame me for the fact that he is not in the mood. Then we fight all night about how he is withholding and again, he blames me. He even makes up the lie that I am the one that says no to his offers of sex. I have NEVER said no to sex. ~Faith

Really skimps on a gift... Dollar store stuff. Or she doesn't buy me anything at all. ~Alice

She filed for divorce on my 40th birthday right in the middle of the surprise birthday party she had thrown for me. Can you imagine the irony? She couldn't be seen as anything but the perfect wife even as she was ending the marriage. ~Carl

He has often said that I am hard to buy for. The bottom line is that buying for me would require that he think about me and actually do something in response. ~Ashley

My birthday was ignored. ~Ciara

He attempted to plan a surprise dinner for me and a few days before just simply came out and told me about it and asked that I finish organizing it. Then he was mad I didn't appreciate his efforts more. I cancelled the whole thing. ~Bev

I threw my own 50th birthday party. Since the kids don't live at home and don't provide him coaching anymore on things like what he should do for a birthday party for me, I knew if I wanted a party, I would have to throw it myself. ~Trina

Vacations

He picks a fight when we're on vacation so there would be no sex. ~Alice

I went on a few with the kids but not with him in recent years. ~Wendy

She doesn't want sex on vacations, and if she does agree to have sex, she does so begrudgingly. I have felt alone on vacations. You pay all this money hoping romance and spontaneous affection could happen and still I get to feel alone. That really stinks. ~Andrew

No matter what vacation we went on, he always would work during them, spending hours on the phone and on his computer. I always felt ignored and frustrated that he couldn't

take a break from working to spend time with me. Finally, we went on two cruises which were good in that he was away from work since his phone didn't work in the middle of the ocean and internet was too expensive for the computer, but he still didn't want to connect much with me. He preferred reading a book by himself. ~Raina

I can make suggestions and we can even do special things but often if we do them it is like being accompanied by a zombie . . . he is there in person but his spirit is missing in action. ~Ashley

I plan vacations, and he vetoes the plans. ~Ciara

He would sit by himself, make no effort to be a part of what was going on but then blame everyone else for not including him. Then he would complain about being anywhere but at home because no one cares about him anyway. ~Ellen

He would go out to party and leave me in the hotel room by myself. ~Bev

Vacations are the classic time for him to complain about everything he can possibly think of and ruin the trip for everyone. ~Trina

Christmas

I get hinting-type gifts, like CD's on being financially responsible or gym memberships. ~Alice

He doesn't help with decorations and only helps with things if I make it a big deal. ~Ashley

He doesn't plan for Christmas. If he gives gifts, they are impulse buys motivated only by his desire to avoid getting in trouble with me. ~Ciara

I get gifts with no meaning and then get blamed for being ungrateful if I returned them. ~Bev

We always lived hand to mouth so we would only buy gifts for the children. If we could afford something, it would be something practical that I did not like. He really didn't care to choose something that I would like. ~Trish

Major Accomplishments

He NEVER recognizes these. Others celebrate me, but he is silent and jokes about his silence. His compliments, when finally offered, are sarcastic. ~Faith

I didn't get a congratulatory call when he knew I was going to be interviewed on TV. ~Alice

Other people would praise me about my accomplishments at church or at work. He's basically uninterested in my accomplishments. ~Wendy

I graduated from a class and had my first performance in front of many of my friends. She didn't bother to show up. Our son was a bit ill and she used the so-called need to stay with him as an excuse for missing my big moment. Our son though could have been watched by someone else. ~Carl

He would give me cards or flowers but then not support me in making our schedule work for my new hours at work. He would put me down for having a university degree but not make as much money as him. ~Bev

He made sure there was nothing to celebrate. If I began do-ing something for myself, he would criticize my attempts regularly until I gave up. The only thing this strategy didn't work on was my giving up counseling and my 12-step meet-ings! ~Trish

Sadly if you're reading these pages you have your own sto-ries of not being celebrated. This lack of celebration on big events can easily be identified. The day in, day out lack of celebration is so strongly felt, so painful.

Again, this is the anorexic's intentional choice not to cel-ebrate you. This lack is not a reflection of your real value.

Chapter Six

Sex

Being married to an intimacy anorexic can present real challenges to their spouses' sexual relationships. Often, an intimacy anorexic—often those of the male persuasion—desires regular sex lives, but the fact that he is often unconnected during sex turns his spouse off such that sex becomes nonexistent.

Sex is to be a beautiful way for two people to celebrate their love and commitment to each other. For those married and alone this beauty is probably not part of the experience period or on any consistent basis. Perhaps sex has been used by your spouse to create distance from you or to inflict pain. Perhaps sex has been used by your spouse to reject you through his or her withholding of sex altogether or through regular rejection of your sexual advances. Perhaps your spouse has even shamed you for desiring sex. Again, this doesn't mean you're not worthy of a great sex life; on the contrary, you are absolutely worthy of the kind of sex life that your spouse is preventing you from having.

As in earlier chapters, here are the responses to our surveys from spouses of intimacy anorexics regarding the interplay between anorexia and sex. Unfortunately some of their experiences may parallel your own. These responses should validate your fledgling belief that your anguish-filled sex life is not your fault. These responses should confirm your understanding that you are not alone in your feelings.

Sexual Relationship

Each night, I cry in bed. I feel so alone when he faces the wall with his back to me. No touching, no talking, no sexuality, no attachment, no connecting. It's very lonely in my bed. I am sad that I cannot share the gift of sex with my husband. I am sad that he is not interested in talking about or sharing this gift with me. I'm sad that he withholds his body. I'm angry that he makes sex about his satisfaction only. I am tired of being shut down when I bring up the subject of sex. I am anxious constantly wondering when will I ever get sex.
~Faith

He didn't touch me for the last 4 years of our marriage.
~Alice

It was never a shared experience but rather "masturbation with a live person—me— to do it". His heart was completely left out of the act. The focus was solely on what felt good physically. Sex became repulsive. He was demanding, showing that sex was only for his gratification. He doesn't understand—or care—that our sexual acts could be something more than they are. I remember crying during sex and he didn't even notice. When I finally kicked him out of the bedroom so I could sleep in peace, he never pursued me. He never communicated that he wanted to be with me, which was one of the last straws for me. ~Wendy

Sex was infrequent at best. She left me to deal with my desires on my own. ~Carl

My husband wasn't interested in sex from the moment we said "I do." For the first few months, I would try to initiate sex but eventually gave up after being turned down so many times and hearing so many excuses. Even when we would be sexual, my husband struggled to get/keep an erection which was frustrating for both of us and I think it made him even less interested in sex with me. ~Raina

I could take this lacking sex life if the emotional and relational sides of our relationship were thriving. I like sex and I enjoy being intimate but I am not willing to give myself sexually and not receive what I need emotionally. I'm not sure if that is a boundary or withholding on my part, but I need to be "known" and "know" the other person before I am willing to enter into a sexual relationship. ~Ashley

He doesn't open his eyes or talk to me during sex. He goes to sleep immediately afterwards, refusing to talk when I want to talk. We have sex only when it is good for him and assumes that I will be available whenever he wants to be intimate. ~Ciara

I felt objectified, like it could be any woman there and he wouldn't know the difference. ~Bev

Eventually, he would masturbate in the shower alone, and I would masturbate while he was in the shower. This came out when we were planning our divorce. ~Trish

Before Sex

I was stressed out. ~Alice

Early years: anticipation, hope.   Later years: dread, fear, depression. ~Wendy

I felt deprived, starved. I would get to the point where I couldn't hold it together any longer. ~Carl

I felt very sexually aroused. I wanted to be sexual with my spouse and to connect with him and feel close to him. ~Raina

We would go about our business as usual, remaining unconnected emotionally and then it was like he believed that after we entered the bedroom, magic dust would fall on me and I would become turned on. ~Ashley

I felt anxious about whether he will accept my invitation. ~Ciara

I usually had a sense of obligation to initiate sex quickly followed by a sense of dread. I felt like he just wanted to get it over with, and I went along with him, hoping that maybe just maybe we might somehow connect before we had sex (which rarely happened). ~Ellen

I felt hopeful and anticipated. ~Trish

During Sex

It's like he is completing a task. The same move every time. Same speed. Same shut downs. Same blames. Same struggle. He has sex with me each time as if he has never been with me and does not know anything about sex. When I give him valuable feedback about what I like, he accuses me of negativity; then he uses that excuse to quit and withhold. When we do have sex, it is boring, painful, rushed, and focused on quickly ejaculating. He acts like I am supposed to really appreciate his sexual gratification while I don't even get touched. ~Faith

I felt insecure. ~Alice

I felt let down, wondering why isn't this working? Why isn't sex with my spouse what it's made out to be? I felt self-hatred and the repulsion of being used as an object. ~Wendy

Longing. I so wanted to connect to her but during sex, I couldn't even see her (the lights had to be out) much less connect with her. Missionary position. No talking. No emotion. ~Carl

Sometimes I felt connected to him, and sometimes I felt like he was in another world—his body was there but his mind was not. ~Raina

There were times of closeness but in general sex always felt like a duty and a duty only for his pleasure, not mine. ~Ashley

He refuses to open his eyes. I don't try to talk because he is hard of hearing and because interruptions seem to frustrate him. ~Ciara

I feel used. It's all about him seeing, feeling, hearing. While he says he wants me to enjoy sex, I don't think it's about me actually enjoying sex but about his arousal at the sight of my enjoyment. ~Ellen

Disappointing. ~Trish

After Sex

The next day he acts like we are total strangers. He will not ask for feedback or give me feedback. He pretends we never had sex. ~Faith

I felt used, raped. I felt like a robot. I felt like a disgusting body or like a fat bridesmaid in a stupid puffy dress whom others compliment only out of pity. ~Alice

I felt disappointed, unfulfilled, and angry. ~Wendy

Exhausted. Despite my best efforts there was still no connection to her. ~Carl

Sometimes I felt very close to him as we would lie there together in each other's arms. But then, he would often go to sleep really quickly and I would be left lying awake. Sometimes I felt very lonely and would cry. ~Raina

Rarely was there cuddling or after chatter or tenderness. ~Ashley

He holds me but doesn't talk to me and he quickly falls asleep. ~Ciara

After sex, I feel grateful to be done. ~Ellen

I felt unfulfilled and extremely desirous of an orgasm. ~Trish

Once in recovery, some intimacy anorexics choose to connect sexually with their spouses. Others, however, choose to continue withholding sex or connection during sex. This **choice to be cruel to you is all about them.**

You absolutely and unequivocally deserve a spouse who will connect with you sexually on a consistent basis. You deserve to be touched, explored and pleasured regularly. If this doesn't shift in early recovery definitely look into getting professional help.

You may also need some help to heal from sexual neglect from your spouse. Your tears and pain are real and your losses from past years or decades are legitimate. So address any of the scarring that may have occurred to your sexuality so that if your spouse does choose true recovery you can join him or her in a healthy sexual future.

Along with the sobering message I have offered, I want to offer a word of hope. I know you have relived some painful moments while reading about the experiences outlined on these pages. In my practice of more than twenty years, I have seen many intimacy anorexics choose healing and restore their marriages completely. I have observed the smiles and the miracles spouses experienced as they talk about their newly recovering spouse and how consistent the intimacy in their marriage has become. If you both heal, much that was damaged in your marriage can be restored.

Chapter Seven

Finding Love?

In this chapter I simply want our fellow travelers on the married-and-alone journey to share their experiences surrounding their quests to find and fight for love with their spouses, including those moments when they reached breaking points. As I did in previous chapters, I am going to simply present their answers to my question as their heartfelt expressions better capture the impact of intimacy anorexia more eloquently than mine ever could.

Define Marital Love

Love is an affection fed by kindness that is given and received by spouses. It is a consuming passion for the well-being of the other that desires only the good of the other. It delights in giving. It is an action and a choice; it is visible. ~Faith

Love is two people being one. ~Alice

Love is doing what is best for your spouse. This may come at great expense to you but is richly rewarding. ~Wendy

Love is not a passive set of words, "I love you." Love for me is sacrifice, commitment, and action. It's the action to put gas in a car for someone else, opening a car door, praying, changing the world of another. ~Carl

Love is a deep connection physically, spiritually, emotionally, and mentally to the point where you want to sacrifice for the other, to serve him or her. ~Raina

It is a connection between only two people that is deeper than friendship. Someone who you share your heart, soul, and body with forsaking all others. ~Ciara

It is not SELF CENTERED. ~Ellen

It is a decision that is characterized by passion. It can be perfectly imperfect such as two people in the marriage. It grows and matures when nurtured. It can be characterized by conflict but also by peace and therefore safety. ~Bev

Marital love is two people trying to out-do each other in their loving actions for each other. In our marriage, we started out this way, but somewhere along the way he stopped performing any loving actions for me though I continued. There is something sick about me that I just blindly continued on out-doing my own loving actions even though they weren't appreciated or reciprocated by my husband. I don't know if what I was doing could even be called love. It was a mechanical response, an incomprehensible one, nothing human. Since I've been in recovery, I'm learning to pay attention to the moment when he stalls in this area and disciplining myself to not go farther or faster than he does. I wish our relationship would advance more, but until he leads us, I'm not going to run ahead of him. I would be embarrassed to try to explain this dynamic to someone, but I am at peace with my decision for I am assured in my heart that this is best for me. ~Trina

Based on your own definition of love, does your spouse love you or not? Why?

Based on my definition, he does not love me. His love was selfish. He loved me in a way that kept his dysfunction going. He loved to be with me so he could keep the anorexia going and justified. Similarly, I justified his victim mentality. ~Faith

My husband did not love me, and even more problematically, he didn't love himself either. And because he didn't love himself, he couldn't love me. ~Alice

No, he doesn't and can't love me. He doesn't even know what love is. ~Wendy

No, she does not love me based on my definition of love (putting one's will at the service of another person) . She doesn't understand love. She can't because she can't love herself. ~Dale

No, he doesn't love me based on the fact that he clearly isn't willing to sacrifice enough to do the hard work of recovery to give our marriage a chance. ~Raina

No, he isn't able to show his love or allow me to know him, and he hasn't been able to give up porn or masturbation. ~Ciara

Sometimes and in some ways his behavior shows he loves me. ~Ellen

What specific efforts have you taken to be loved? Did they work?

I work really hard at being perfect, getting everything done so all he has left to do is love me. I do all of the traditional woman's jobs around the house as well as the man's (his) jobs and I do them perfectly and efficiently so I can get noticed. But he neither notices nor says "thank you." I make my husband's life so simple that all he has to do is go to work and come home to love me. But he still avoids and ignores me. No kiss when he comes home, no touch, no sex, no appreciation, no valuing. The more he ignores me though the harder I work to make him notice me. ~Faith

I tried looking good. I tried earning lots of money. I tried being a super mom. I tried creating a beautiful home. I tried making delicious meals. I tried placing meals made by gourmet chefs in my pans (as if I had cooked the meals). I tried working hard. I tried being a good sex partner. I tried everything I could think of. But I failed. Then I tried leaving him. And guess what? I was so happy! ~Alice

I tried to communicate my needs in various ways. I role-played, hinted, talked in person, talked on the phone, emailed, sent letters and cards. I sought help from outside sources such as counselors, Bible studies, workbooks, videos, etc. I had many children in hopes he would praise me. I cooked great meals. I counseled him, prayed with him, submitted to him. I looked up to him and had high hopes for him and told him so. I did what books said to do. I did what counselors said to do. Oh God, I gave it my all. But he never loved me in return. ~Wendy

I kept trying to remove the barriers she complained about. She was too tired from cleaning the house, so I hired a house cleaner. She said I had an anger problem, I sought help. She said I didn't have a good enough relationship with our son, so I worked on it. We had date nights and special times to connect each night. I'd do special things for her like leaving her notes. I wrote her a "brag book" of affirmations. If it was something to try ... I tried it. ~Carl

I thought if I was successful she would love me. Then she told me she would love me if we were debt fee. I jumped through both hoops but still didn't get loved. So I tried other things: I did housework and gave her extended quality time or touch but still nothing worked. No matter how extravagant my attempts to love her, I still didn't get love or affection in return. ~Andrew

I tried to help my spouse in various ways in order to be loved by him. Unfortunately, I think the more I tried to help him, the more he saw me as a smother mother and the more he resented me. I also sought love by initiating sex and by wearing sexy lingerie, for the most part, he just wasn't interested in sex with me. I think in a way I tried to be loved by checking up on his computer all the time so that he wouldn't look at porn and would look at me and be interested in me but instead he just stopped viewing porn at home and started viewing it at work. ~Raina

I am naturally a great helper. . . working alongside the other, anticipating needs. So I brought that ability into the marriage. I made sure that things around the house were in order so he could relax when he got home. I would "submit," even when I had grave doubts about what he was wanting to do because I thought that was the "good Christian" thing to do.

I thought if I forgave quickly that trust would be restored quickly but I was left with unanswered questions and resentment because he hadn't changed. I took responsibility for more than my part of situations. I found myself making excuses for him, why he didn't get things done, or didn't care for me the way others did. ~Ashley

I raised his son, managed the whole house, entertained friends, had sex when I didn't want to, changed jobs to make things easier for our routine and him, supported his business choices despite my discomfort with some of them, trusted him and forgave him after I caught him cheating, begged him to ask about me and my life, disciplined the kids on my own, looked after his needs before my own, helped him with issues around his dad and ex-wife, managed the kids' educations, gave surprise parties for him, and booked marriage counseling. I wasn't loved for these acts and in some cases he used them against me. His lack of response to my seemingly endless acts of love created a sense of chaos and confusion in me that left me reeling. ~Bev

I tried to be sexy or dress sexy which worked only temporarily. I tried to be understanding and supportive but was still unloved. Helped with cleaning his work truck….unloved. Cleaned the house…unloved. Did things around the house to make it nicer…unloved. Wrote and hid little notes around the house telling him how much I loved him or that he was handsome…unloved. Played with his hair while we drove in the car… unloved. Gave him massages…unloved. I played and flirted…unloved, again. Nothing worked, period. ~Trish

How did you get the love you wanted?

An ultimatums: Go to counseling or we are done. ~Faith

Oh, if he knew I was pissed off completely and got really mad, then he would try to show love at least for a little while. ~Alice

I never got the love I wanted and needed. He might try to be nicer than usual, but that was usually to get sex. ~Wendy

I described it as walking through a carnival house of glass walls. Once I'd figure out how to help her understand my love for her (which she mostly rejected) I'd feel like I had found a path through the fun house. However, she would then change the location of the glass walls. I'd run into something new, some new problem and that gave her an excuse to not demonstrate her love for me. ~Carl

The only thing that caused her to show love was my threatening to leave or my mirroring her behavior for a couple of days. All of these were highly costly for me emotionally speaking, so even if they worked for a week or so they cost me so much. ~Andrew

I would sometimes get mad about how he was treating me and we would argue and then he might try a little harder to be sexual or closer to me for a little while but then he was right back to his normal self pretty quickly. ~Raina

Sex would bring us close for a while. ~Ciara

I would allow things to build and build until the pressure became too much and I complained. He'd respond to my complaint and I'd see a more intimate side of him for a short period of time—long enough to trick me into thinking he'd changed. But he never had. ~Bev

What are examples of you reaching a breaking point?

Finding phone calls to a female coworker when he swore he had not been calling her. Going without sex for an entire year. ~Faith

I felt insanity slipping in and then became afraid that I would lose our children. ~Alice

She tried blaming me for her missing a commitment, a charge I was innocent of. ~Carl

I felt that I no longer wanted to go on. I felt no desire and no sense of purpose, like I had bought into his plan of laziness. ~Ashley

We attended counseling together to address his lack of sexual attraction to me. The counseling was really going nowhere. Then for various reasons I cleared my calendar and stayed home three Thursday nights in a row. (I usually work on Thursday nights.) Nothing was on the agenda and still there was neither sex nor intimacy coming towards me. On the third Friday morning I woke up when he was getting ready for work and told him I wanted a separation. ~Trina

Have you reached the final breaking point?

Yes. I filed for divorce 2 times. But each time, he came back around, got help and became temporarily getting involved in our marriage. ~Faith

I did move out and was done with him. My leaving forced my husband to go to Heart to Heart Counseling Center and get the help he needed. ~Alice

Yes, I'm thinking of filing for divorce in January but I have to weigh it with how much stress the filing itself will create and whether this is the best time. ~Wendy

Yes, we have been separated for 4 years. In my mind, I am ready to divorce, but for some reason, I am struggling to make the call to the lawyer. ~Raina

I believe I have reached breaking points at different times throughout the journey. ~Ashley

No because he is working on his issues and I am working on mine. ~Ciara

I am starting to reach my breaking point. I thought a lot of the anorexic behaviors would lessen in frequency and intensity the longer he was sober. There have indeed been many improvements, but as I become healthier I also see more of his passive-aggression and they are preventing us from drawing closer now that I'm healing from the trauma of learning about his anorexia. ~Bev

Yes, I've reached the breaking point several times. Each time he gets it together for a short time and loves me like I want, but lasting change didn't finally come until I detached completely from him. My detachment created a real in-house separation. I had a clear and written vision for behavior to support restoration of the marriage that I would need to see happening before reattaching. It was a very slow and lonely process, but he eventually rose to the challenge. I had to stand strong and not buy into his talk and not compromise by being satisfied with anything less. When we got married we both vowed to express our love in many ways and so we could have lots of sex. I had to remember that this was still the purpose for our marriage. ~Trina

Trying to find love while being married to an intimacy anorexic who doesn't choose recovery is challenging to say the least. I think you can hear in the voices of our responders the scars of this ache to be loved, this failure to be loved. In the section that follows, we can hear the same ache in respondents' testimonies of how they feel changed by their spouses' anorexia.

I became withdrawn. I lied to protect him. I felt ashamed of being a person with needs. I felt grotesque. ~Alice

I am less hopeful and positive and more depressed. I am more inclined to give up easily but more compassionate. ~*Wendy*

It's like parts of me are dying. I don't have the same zest for living having been uncelebrated and denied affection for so long. I feel unwanted, criticized, and less attractive. ~Andrew

It did have negative effects on me as I was thinking about having an affair and I think I began to equate sex with love. I became more and more distant from my husband and I was angry all the time. I found myself taking my anger out on my daughter. Still, lately I am changing for the positive: I am learning to see myself as beautiful the way God sees me. So even though I wouldn't have chosen an intimacy anorexic/sexually addicted spouse, God has used this experience to grow and change me for the better. ~Raina

I have been so much more adept at reading people and being alert to potential problems in relationships. I don't fear asking tough questions like I used to. Because of my heartbreaking experiences with my husband, I feel called to bind up the broken hearted, and the spouses of anorexics are

truly broken hearted. Living with these painful experiences doesn't make me a saint, it just means I am more compassionate. ~Ashley

I have become more compassionate. In addition, I have grown up, becoming much more independent now than when I entered the relationship. I cope better and grieve more easily. ~Ciara

I had become codependent, controlling, bitter, critical, and reactive to my intimacy anorexic. Those traits are all but gone now thanks to God and my recovery work. ~Bev

Chapter Eight

Married to Themselves

I am a champion for and true believer in marriage as demonstrated through my professional activities and my personal life. I love marriage and I want the world to know! Despite my great love and admiration for marriage, then, why is this chapter one of the most challenging experiences I've had in my writing career?

In short, I see the dangers to a good marriage. I see what threatens and often destroys marriage. Despite my sincere desire that every marriage succeed, I recognize the reality that both spouses must be healthy or working toward health. If such conditions do not exist, though, a marriage will quickly come under attack. Still, a sincere desire to move toward health can cover a multitude of sins, so to speak. Marriages riddled with addictions and trauma (for example, sex addiction, intimacy anorexia, anger, control, etc) can still become healthy, thriving marriages with the right attitude paired with some good old-fashioned hard work.

In some cases, however, one person can be so selfish and so unwilling to work on his or her issues, often including intimacy anorexia, that the marriage's survival is in danger. The danger is due to the anorexics lack of honor and devotion toward their marriage. In our survey involving spouses of anorexia, we asked two questions related to the issue of unfaithfulness. Now in the survey we were not addressing sexual unfaithfulness as most intimacy anorexics don't want sex with someone other than their spouses (The exception would be the anorexic who is also a sex addict). The unfaithfulness we address in our survey is the anorexic's failure to keep his or her wedding vow to honor, love and respect his or her spouse.

This unfaithfulness exists when one spouse is married more to him or herself or to an addiction of choice than to his or her spouse. Intimacy anorexics love, honor, and cherish themselves and their need for safety and control.

In the book *Addicted to Adultery: The Other Reason Spouses Cheat* (Discovery Press, 2010), I include questions to help individuals identify emotional unfaithfulness in their spouses. These questions get at the heart of the issue: does the he love me or his addiction? Does she prefer me or her selfishness? As you read through these questions below, listen to your gut. Then acknowledge your gut responses honestly.

Threat #1
Does the Intimacy Anorexic Love Me?

1. Behavior
___ Is the intimacy anorexic's behavior congruent with a desire to recover?
___ Is the intimacy anorexic completing his or her workbooks, attending groups or therapy?

2. Protection

___ Is the intimacy anorexic honest about his or her addiction or secretive?

___ Is the intimacy anorexic being honest about small relapses?

3. Perspective

___ Are your spouse's ideas about you positive?

___ Is the intimacy anorexic discovering the positive sides of recovery?

4. Motivation

___ Do you see the intimacy anorexic employing creativity in the recovery process?

___ Do you see the intimacy anorexic increasing in his or her knowledge about the recovery process?

___ Do you see the intimacy anorexic involving others in his or her recovery?

5. Humility

___ Do you see acceptance of responsibility for your spouse's actions?

___ Do you see genuine gratefulness sustained over time?

Love for Anorexia?

1. Behavior

___ Does the intimacy anorexic make excuses not to follow a plan for recovery?

___ Does the intimacy anorexic still lie?

___ Is the intimacy anorexic sneaky?

___ Does the intimacy anorexic refuse to be accountable?

2. Protection

___ Will the intimacy anorexic only admit to wrong-doing after being caught?

___ Does the intimacy anorexic participate in anorexic be haviors with no display of guilt or of concern?

3. Perspective

___ Does the intimacy anorexic rationalize how their life could have been better without you?

___ Does the intimacy anorexic still talk about the anorexia?

___ Does the grief of losing the intimacy anorexia cause greater pain than does the devastation wrought by the anorexia?

4. Motivation

___ Does the intimacy anorexic skip group and therapy ap-pointments?

___ Does the intimacy anorexic get angry about the inconvenience recovery work is having on his or her life?

5. Humility

___ Does the intimacy anorexic speak and/or behave arro gantly?

___ Does the intimacy anorexic attribute his or her pain to you, his or her spouse?

___ Does the intimacy anorexic still express an attitude of entitlement?

After looking at these questions what conclusions have you drawn? What have you come to believe? Take a moment to seriously think about and deeply feel what seems to be really true about your relationship. Some of you might re-alize that your spouse does really love you and is trying to heal in order to love you more. Others might realize that their spouses are in love with themselves only. Whether the reality of your marital situation brings grief or rejoicing, acknowledging this reality is an important step for you. The refusal to honestly acknowledge reality will only allow a dysfunctional relationship to remain dysfunctional.

Threat #2
Addictions

I am a recovering addict so I have real knowledge and understanding of addictions. In addition to knowledge gleaned through experience, I have gained knowledge through years of training about various addictions such that I am now the President of the American Association for Sex Addiction Therapy having worked primarily with sex addicts and intimacy anorexics during the entirety of my clinical career.

Understanding addiction, I can tell you that an addiction is **a disease based on the addict's choice to be addicted.** Even if the addiction is the indirect result of childhood abuse or **some other factor out of the addict's control, the choice to** partake daily in addictive behavior is still 100% a choice. And this choice is a progressive one meaning that each time an individual chooses to act upon the addiction, he or she ensures that his or her healing process from the addiction **will be longer and more arduous.**

A twenty year old who has been an addict for five years has given more of herself to her addiction than a fifty year old who has been an addict for 10 years. Over time, like a drop of black ink in a bowl of clear water, the addiction more and more obscures who the addict truly is and even takes her over. A Chinese proverb on this explains it succinctly:

First a man takes a drink.
Then a drink takes a drink.
Then the drink takes the man.

So it is with intimacy anorexia. A twenty year old soul is less damaged by intimacy anorexia choices and less entrenched than a fifty or sixty year old soul.

Addicts remain underdeveloped emotionally, spiritually and morally. Most anorexics are adolescents at best and children at worst when it comes to emotions, morals, and the spiritual. One clear sign of this arrested development is the anorexic's inability to see you, the spouse, as an amazing person of worth and value but instead as an object or something to be disdained. Not someone. Something.

So why might you, the spouse, have stayed with an intimacy anorexic for all these years? Well, you're like the proverbial frog in the slow boiling water. The anorexia gets ever so slightly worse year after year and year after year, you adapt, jump through the latest hoop, until one day you wake up with the horrible realization that decades of being unloved have just about choked the very life out of you.

Threat #3
Protection Principle

Over the many years counseling addicts I have discovered some principles that can quickly and clearly illuminate whether a man or woman really wants to recover from addiction. One of these principles is called the protection principle.

According to this simple yet profoundly accurate principle,

what a person loves is what he or she protects. Think about it for a moment. Who are the people you would protect if threatened? It's the people you love.

When the anorexic loves himself or is being ~Faithful to only himself, he protects his anorexic behaviors from threats. When he loves you, on the other hand, he protects you and fights for his health and for your relationships. I have seen countless men and women grab their swords and slice off the intimacy anorexia tentacles that have been slowly choking the relationship and in the process, becoming the great spouses they desire to be. These are the heroes.

I have also seen the tragedies where the anorexic picks up their sword only to turn on her spouse, protecting her anorexia instead. These individuals are truly married to themselves, having freely chosen this path.

My hope is that discussing the threats to a marriage and whether the anorexic wants to be married to you or to the anorexia has been helpful. You are empowered when you know and accept your spouse's decision.

Chapter Nine

Real Recovery

Recovery from intimacy anorexia is possible for those who want to heal. However, unlike alcohol, food addiction or even sexual addiction, recovery from intimacy anorexia is not achieved by simply stopping a behavior; it is a changing of a way of being, a changing of a nature that withholds into a nature that gives, a changing from passivity to active giving.

As the spouse of an intimacy anorexic, you need to know exactly what recovery looks like for the anorexic. Seeing these basic recovery steps can give you the strength you will need to endure throughout the process, even through relapses. Knowing the end goal and the definite possibility of reaching that goal, there can be hope. However, without knowing and practicing these basic recovery steps, there is little chance of true recovery.

Recovery from intimacy anorexia means that the anorexic spouse begins to actively connect with you emotionally, spiritually and sexually. If he or she is indeed connecting (through the use of the exercises and strategies outlined in this chapter), then you have great reason to hope! Your spouse has reached sobriety. If, however, he or she is not actively pursuing and connecting to you, he or she is not sober but instead in a state of relapse and/or non-recovery.

Recovery with You

As a spouse you deserve to know if your anorexic spouse is going to stop withholding after years of this behavior. If the intimacy anorexic completes another year of therapy but doesn't connect you are now another year more deprived of intimacy with intentional pain in your life. Measuring your spouse's sobriety from intimacy anorexia can give both of you a clear picture of what the anorexic is truly choosing. Remember, all addicts choose what they want, whether it's recovery or addictive behaviors.

Three Dailies

The Three Dailies is the first recovery step, a practice that gets at the core of what is ailing the intimacy anorexic. Your spouse is to do all these exercises with you; however, you are not to initiate them. Your letting your spouse initiate is of the utmost importance. If the intimacy anorexic, refuses to initiate these exercises, he or she has likely relapsed and is no longer in recovery from his intimacy anorexia.

Initiating is a necessary part of the anorexics' healing; don't rob them of this important step. Keep this in mind: you cannot make the Three Dailies happen. Allow and encourage your spouse to initiate, but if this initiating doesn't happen, know that your spouse is rejecting intimacy and choosing anorexia. You, as a spouse may have to face the hard truth that your anorexic spouse may not really want intimacy with you. Hard as it may be, you deserve to know the truth.

The first of the Three Dailies is the feelings exercise, an exercise that will at first be challenging, but like with many initially challenging activities, will become easier over time. Start with the sentence frames below.

I feel _____ when _____ (This is the present tense).
I first remember feeling _____ when _____ (This example is under the age of 18).

Then, locate the list of feelings found in the Appendix. Each day, you will choose a feeling at random; your spouse will do the same. Then, taking turns—with the intimacy anorexic going first, place your chosen emotion word in the first blank and finish the sentence honestly.

The purpose of this activity is to help both spouses learn to identify their different emotions with the larger goal of helping them to communicate emotional intimacy to each other. As you practice intentional communicating of feelings from your heart you and your spouse are moving toward sobriety since it counteracts the intentional withholding of emotion that is typical of intimacy anorexia. When doing this exercise, make sure you follow these three simple rules in order to keep the exercise safe for both of you.

Rule #1: No examples ever about your spouse or the marriage may be used.

Rule #2: Maintain eye contact during the exercise.

Rule #3: No feedback should be provided to the other's sharing. Simply listen.

You will do the feelings exercise just this way daily for 90 days. After the 90 days, you will continue the exercise in a different way, using feelings you experienced that day to "fill in the blanks" rather than feelings from the list in the Appendix, continuing this practice for the duration of your marriage. After 90 days you no longer will need to complete the sentence as to when you first remember feeling this.

So that you know what to expect, eyes wide open, you need to be aware of what an intimacy anorexic's attempt to sabotage the first exercise might look like. The spouse more committed to anorexia than recovery might sabotage by:

1) Just not initiating
2) Making excuses so as to avoid the consequence agreed upon
3) Being trite or trivial during exercises
4) Remaining cerebral
5) Refusing to maintain eye contact with the spouse; refusing to talk directly to the spouse

The second exercise also encourages emotional connection. One of the characteristics of intimacy anorexia is focusing inordinately on the flaws of the spouse. A related characteristic is the tendency to withhold praise. This exercise directly addresses these two characteristics as it requires the **spouse to give two compliments to each other, things you** love, like or appreciate about each other.

Going first, the intimacy anorexic initiates eye contact with the spouse and then says, "Name, I really love, like, appreciate (pick one) about you." The receiving spouse must

then—and this is very important—make a conscious effort
to receive that praise and really let it in. When the receiving spouse has fully received the praise, he or she may say
"Thank you." Then, the receiving spouse becomes the initiating spouse, dispensing praise. And so on until both of you
have given and received two praises from each other.

The third exercise involves praying together. Regardless of
your beliefs, you pray out loud together, taking turns. The
intent of this exercise is to counteract the intimacy anorexic's tendency to withhold spiritual intimacy. It is, therefore,
an essential piece for healing.

Make sure these three exercises are completed daily. It
might be a good idea to note in writing the frequency of
completion for your own ability to observe change in your
spouse's behavior.

Let's recap.

• 3 Dailies
• Feelings shared (2 each)
• Praises given (2 each)
• Verbal Prayers (1 each)
• Each activity done daily at a set time
• Establish a consequence if the intimacy anorexic does not
  initiate these exercises
• Monitor sabotaging behavior

The anorexic also will need to set consequences for him
or herself for not completing initiation of the Three Dailies. Some self-imposed consequences might be not-often-
enjoyed tasks like cleaning the toilets or tasks that don't
benefit them directly (but might benefit you) like a 30 minute shoulder rub.

Sexual Agreement

A sexual agreement is the second of these three recovery
steps, the second leg of the recovery stool, so to speak. The
first recovery step addressed emotional and spiritual intimacy. This second step addresses sexual intimacy. Here,
you are working toward connectedness during sex. Like
sabotaging behaviors appearing in response to the feelings
exercises, the sexual agreement exercises might evoke attempts to sabotage. The sabotaging behaviors you might
find include the following:

1) Not keeping the commitment to have sex
2) Disconnecting during sex
3) Negative communication before, during, or after sex
4) Using an anorexic characteristic to keep the spouse from
   desiring sex
5) Refusing to accept consequences

The appearance of these sabotaging behaviors indicates the
strong affinity the anorexic has to withholding from his or
her spouse. Still, with patience and perseverance, a sexual
agreement can be reached and practiced.

There are three components to a sexual agreement: agreeing about frequency of sexual intercourse, agreeing about a
schedule of initiation, and setting consequences for breaking these agreements. The first component is the estab-
lishment of a frequency of sexual intercourse. If you're
under 50, 2-3 times a week is a good number to shoot
for, and if you're over 50, 1-2 times a week would be aver-
age. In almost no circumstance should frequency of sexual
intercourse drop below one time a week. It is also important to note that spouses should discuss sexual intercourse
as it intersects with the woman's menstrual cycle, coming

to an agreement.

Now that both of you have established a desired sexual frequency, it is time to split initiation responsibilities. This responsibility for initiation of sexual intercourse should be split 50/50 in any way you and your spouse see fit. It is a good idea to build flexibility into your schedule such that a particular spouse might have two days in which to initiate sex one time, such as a Monday and Tuesday range in which sexual intercourse should happen once. You might decide that each of you will be responsible for initiating sex on particular days that you can agree on. You might decide that one spouse will initiate on Monday, Tuesday, and Wednesday and the other will initiate on Thursday, Friday, and Saturday with Sunday as an "off day."

In the Rotation of Weeks Schedule, one person gets weeks one and three. The second person gets weeks two and four. You both initiate the frequency you agreed to and rotate the weeks for who initiates sex.

Let me take a moment to talk about special cases surrounding initiating; if this is difficult to understand, see the detailed exercises in the Intimacy Anorexia Workbook. If the intimacy anorexic normally rarely initiates sex, then for the first 60 days the intimacy anorexic should do all the initiating of sex, in order to build up his ability to initiate. If both are intimacy anorexics, neither prone to initiating, they might flip a coin to decide who will initiate this month and who the next, etc.

If both spouses are right away following through with initiating half the time, great! However, if the intimacy anorexic is slacking and not living up to his or her end of the bargain, seek professional help.

Now to the third aspect of a sexual agreement: setting up consequences for breaking the agreements.

Each person sets up their own consequences for not keeping their sexual agreements. For the intimacy anorexic the **consequence needs to be extremely severe as the anorexic** uses withholding of sex to intentionally create pain for his or her spouse. He or she, requires a strong deterrent from this negative behavior. Here are some of consequences anorexics have set for themselves:

• Half day's wage donated to the political party they oppose
• Sleeping in the garage with only a blanket for warmth and comfort
• Cooking for the family for a week
• Giving his wife $200 to go to the spa or her husband $200 for golf
• One month no television or computer use

Any consequence will do; it just needs to be painful for the anorexic not for the sake of punishing the anorexic but for the sake of breaking the cycle of negative and hurtful behavior.

We covered what the intimacy anorexic and the spouse need to do together in order for optimal recovery for the intimacy anorexic spouse. Now I want to give a window into what are individual practices for the intimacy anorexic necessary for optimal recovery. Though these activities are completed individually, it is still helpful for you both to agree **on the frequency which these behaviors will be completed** **so you are both on the same page.**

5 Commandments

I want to first introduce you to what have come to be known as the "5 C's", short for the five commandments. These are five exercises that the intimacy anorexic does daily (except for attending meetings) for the first 90 days of recovery.

Commandment #1: Pray

Regardless of the presence of personal ~Faith or its lack, prayer is an important way for the anorexic to start the day in recovery. This prayer might be as simple as, "God, help me give love to my spouse. Keep my heart open as I heal, and any other help you can offer would be great." Whether or not you are familiar with prayer, just keep it honest, authentic, not a memorized mantra that you repeat without feeling. This prayer is just you opening up your heart to God and asking for some help on the road to recovery today.

Commandment #2: Read

Read recovery literature about intimacy anorexia such as Intimacy Anorexia: Healing the Hidden Addiction in Your Marriage, Leadership and Self Deception, Anatomy of Peace, and Bonds That Make Us Free. In the case where you can't access one of these titles, almost any book on marriage or intimacy would do. These would be good follow-up books for anorexia recovery. Reading daily helps the anorexic stay focused on the goal of actively initiating emotional, spiritual and sexual intimacy with his or her spouse.

Commandment #3: Meetings

Since intimacy anorexia is the youngest member to the Twelve Step family, its groups are few and far between. A national director of intimacy anorexia groups does exist, however. Call Heart to Heart Counseling Center at 719-278-3708 to access this national directory. In the case that a local group can't be found, you might consider starting your own group. If this is true for you, see the Appendix of this book for instructions for structuring your group.

Another option for those who can't find local groups is a therapist-led telephone support group. The therapists that lead these telephone support groups are trained through AASAT (American Association for Sex Addiction Therapy), currently the only organization that is training therapists to treat intimacy anorexia.

To attend a telephone group, you simply call in at the group's scheduled time. There you will "meet" 6-8 people of your same sex who are also intimacy anorexics; this is your support group. During the group, the members cover the workbook exercises that were completed that week from Intimacy Anorexia: The Workbook and Intimacy Anorexia: The Steps. They give each other feedback and then focus on that week's topic.

Commandment #4: Phone Calls

Members of the same group call each other daily for the first 90 days in order to check in on progress of initiating the 3 Dailies and sex, any withholding characteristics (the 10), or any other specific strategies that members are working on. During these phone calls, both members share and both members offer support.

Calls are one of the most tale-tell signs of an intimacy anorexic's recovery or lack thereof. If intimacy anorexics are not making calls, they are relying on themselves to recover, a technique which these intimacy anorexics have proven to fail. Calls made, however, can show a willingness to rely on others and a seriousness about recovery.

Commandment #5: Pray Again
Any day free of anorexic behaviors beats a day of withhold-ing. Therefore, in the evening, the intimacy anorexic is to take a moment and thank God for a sober day. God deserves thanks for helping anorexics live the miracle of recovery to-ward initiating intimacy toward you, the spouse.
To review, the 5 C's to recovery are:

• Pray
• Read
• Meetings
• Calls
• Pray Again

Factors Indicating Progress Toward Recovery

The following are road markers to indicate whether the an-orexic is actually in recovery. These are simple ideas that can serve as a quick checklist to reference in order to deter-mine the anorexic's direction, whether he or she is on the right road.

1. Intimacy Anorexics Do What They Want to Do
Intimacy anorexics do not behave as they do because they are lacking in motivation. Instead, they have plenty of moti-vation, motivation to do what they want and only what they want, even if this behavior is self-destructive. Nobody can stop them when they put their mind to something.

2. Believe Behavior
Intimacy anorexics can talk a really good game, expressing what I call verbal reality. If they say it, it is true; if they say it with emotional vibrato, it is really true. However, they don't feel obligated to follow through so that their words and their actions are not consistent.

3. Creativity

I just told you intimacy anorexics of all kinds are self motivated. If they want to do something, they don't need goad-
ing to get something done; they just do it. Inherent in their
actions is a kind of creativity.

One of the ways I can determine if intimacy anorexics are in
recovery is by following their creativity. Are they being creative when their schedule changes so that they can get the
3 dailies done? Are they keeping their sexual agreement
and calling their group members, or is their creativity being used for excuse making and responsibility avoiding? You
may have heard the phrase, "follow the money" but with intimacy anorexics it's, "follow the creativity" and you'll know
the truth.

4. Groups and Calls

Since initiating intimacy is difficult, I know that anorexics
who are making their calls daily and attending groups are
really stretching themselves. The level to which an anorexic is stretching himself is the level to which he is showing
that he can do what it takes to heal. And the reverse is true
for those who will choose their comfort zones over their
spouses, again and again, rather than letting themselves
be stretched. If the former case is true, the anorexic is on
the road toward healing. If the latter is true, the anorexic is
stuck, unwilling or unable to change.

Honesty About Relapses

For intimacy anorexics, a relapse is not a cause for despair,
for if an intimacy anorexic slips but is honest about that slip,
progress is still being made. Forward motion is still happening. Remember, sharing flaws is hard work. Learning new
patterns of behavior can be terrifying. So, the fact that the

Real Recovery   135

anorexic is putting forth positive effort is a great sign. In the case, though of a relapse, if the anorexic can self-identify and admit the negative behavior, all is well. If you are still spending a lot of time convincing the intimacy anorexic that she is withholding, then she has likely left the path to recovery.

Quick to Complete Designated Consequences

When an intimacy anorexic finds him or herself withholding, pushing away, not following sexual agreements and failing to do The Three Dailies, consequences must be completed to correct the negative behavior. The intimacy anorexic completing these consequences quickly and without complaint is also a positive sign.

Emotional Thawing

Emotional thawing is not something an intimacy anorexic can fake. This effect is a sure sign that the anorexic is doing his or her work necessary for recovery. Emotional thawing is the effect that results in the anorexic experiencing more feelings and experiencing each feeling more intensely.

Leaning Toward

Lastly, a specific behavior I see with intimacy anorexics in recovery is what I call leaning toward. In anorexia, when intimacy anorexics gets hurt, they pull away or push others away. Leaning in is the opposing action, the action of an anorexic remaining in the pain or actually moving toward it in order to maintain connection with loved ones.

Your Recovery

Intimacy anorexia affects each marriage quite differenly, but common to all marriages involving anorexics: the spouse never escapes unscathed. I highly recommend that you consider a journey of healing from the effects of your spouse's intimacy anorexia. You may be facing big decisions regarding the future of your marriage relationship that impact you and your children. You will need to be as healthy as possible as you make the decisions that are ahead of you.

Chapter Ten

Staying

"Dr. Weiss, should I stay?" The question comes up on a regular basis in my therapy sessions. **The answer to that question depends on the couple and situation. It is unique from case to case.**

However the journey to answering that question starts at **the beginning with what was once hoped for. So let's start there. At the end of this journey in this chapter I will share** some key thoughts to consider if your spouse is working his **or her recovery.**

What is the story you hoped for?

I thought we would grow old together and be a support for each other and have joy. ~Alice

I thought we would be best friends and that our intimacy would grow over the years. I thought that our bond would deepen, that our experiences would only become more rich.

I thought he would be a respected man active in the church. I thought he would be a good dad. I thought we would have fun together and accomplish great things. ~Wendy

I wanted a life partner. Someone with whom I could share my life: the joy, the pain, the hopes, the fears. ~Carl

I wanted a fun love affair with my best friend involving fun sex. I want to create time to be together without the kids sometimes and to celebrate each other and encourage each other in their dreams. ~Andrew

I hoped to be loved, cared for, and cherished. ~Faith

I wanted a marriage where we would be close emotionally, intellectually, and sexually. I wanted a marriage where we would pray together and read the Bible together. I wanted to have both common and individual interests. I wanted a marriage where Christ was the center. I wanted a marriage where I felt cherished and pursued, where I could trust and be trusted. Where we could both be ourselves and both be loved. I wanted a life where we would enjoy raising our children together, to love God and each other well. ~Raina

I wanted a connection with a man I love that would allow us to share pain, sorrow, joy, and intimacy in a free way that brings us closer. A relationship that is based on honesty and centered on a loving God. ~Ciara

I wanted a happy and mutually supportive marriage with someone who knows me better than I know myself. I wanted to raise our kids, go to church, have successful careers, build a home, laugh regularly and often, have regular and meaningful sex, show mature love, and live deeply within a relationship with God. ~Bev

I wanted to have a completely mutually supportive partner, friend, and lover. I wanted to give and receive love in a warm-hearted, fun way, with much laughter and love of life. I want us to explore God, the world, and life together. To parent side-by-side as a unit, backing each other up, raising our children to love God and love others. To have a wonderful fulfilling life and sex life through retirement and old age. ~Trish

What is the story you have now?

While he was sick, life with him was a nightmare. He did get better through therapy, however, and because of lots of work, sacrifice, and learning, now life with him is a dream. We are so happy, so in love, so together, so motivated and at peace. We are more in love than ever before. ~Alice

We aren't even friends, much less best friends. We never really bonded since to bond you must open yourself up, and he never opened himself up. When I did open myself up, I was met with nothing to attach to. Living on the surface doesn't lead to rich experiences or deep conversations. I could count on one hand the number of dates we've been on since married. The lack of relationship has held me back from accomplishing much of anything except for raising children, but I do have hopes for what God will do through me, and how He will use my pain for good. Still, I look forward to getting out from under the heartache and neglect. ~Wendy

I was ignored, rejected, and denied love. ~Faith

Fragmented. Disconnected. Unappreciated. Condemned. I feel like I have a millstone around my neck which prevents me from being happy. ~Carl

Our relationship was just not affectionate, creative, or much fun. We support each other in projects but I feel married and alone too often. ~Andrew

I have a husband with two addictions (sexual and intimacy anorexic) who would rather look at porn and masturbate or go to a prostitute than have sex with me. I can count on two hands the number of times we have had sexual intercourse in the last 12 years leaving me feeling distant and alone, upset and even used. We have been separated for 4 years and we would be divorced if I could just get myself to take that next step. I have a marriage where all we basically talk about is our daughter. I have a marriage where there is no connection—physically, emotionally, or spiritually. I now realize that I have the same type of bad marriage that my parents had (my mom has come to realize that my dad is an intimacy anorexic through my recovery work), exactly the type of marriage I so desperately wanted to avoid. ~Raina

I have a committed friend who loves me the best way he can. He is committed to staying married and to working on the marriage in his time frame and in his own way. I enjoy doing things with him. I love his family and he loves mine. We love each other. ~Ciara

I have a husband who conned me into not seeing how anorexic he was. He allowed me to do all the work and I gladly accepted that responsibility. He cheated on me with many women and pornography; he lied and didn't support me emotionally—and then he got caught. After he was caught, he became sober, admitting all the details and that thrust us both into recovery. Recovery has brought such positive change! We've reconnected with God in a way I have never experienced. Sex is more meaningful. He's aware of the IA behaviors and is trying to work on them (this has been way more difficult for him than staying sober in his SA). I have learned a ton about myself, grown, healed and continue to pursue healing and God. I've started a new career that my husband supports, and my kids appear happier. The cycle is being and will ultimately be broken. ~Bev

I was naïve and married a lame husband. As a counselor said, "he was an extreme case of an intimacy anorexic." He broke my heart, my spirit, and my life apart. However, I received help and am getting back on track. Now I can honestly say that the experience does not define who I am today. I am still learning and growing in my recovery from the insane abuse I endured; I am learning to improve my relationships day by day, and learned to believe behavior! Now I recognize unhealthy men quickly and have hope that one day, I may get married again. Either way, I am enjoying a successful life now. I'm in exc~Ellent hands. I own my own home, am getting my bachelors' degree and two quarters ago I made the deans' list and I'm still on it!! ~Trish

Are intimacy anorexics married to themselves?

Yes. If there is a need, he will meet it very selfishly. I am treated like I don't exist and that I have no needs. It's all about getting his needs met immediately and now. ~Faith

Oh for sure! He always came first. He is the most selfish and childish person I have ever met. ~Alice

Sure. Everything revolves around him. He is unable to apologize and make amends because to do so would require him to admit that he failed. He can't see how his actions affect others; his only concern is the effect of his actions on himself. ~Wendy

Yes, but it's not that clear-cut. Her behavior is pretty passive-aggressive. She gets what she wants by agreeing with my requests then never following through. She doesn't know what she wants, so she can't really give herself what she wants. She can't ask for what she wants. There's a Bangles song, "If she knew what she wants – he'd be giving it to her." ~Carl

My husband is so very selfish. One great example of his selfishness came when I first started recovery. One day he said, "That's nice that you are learning. But what are they teaching you about how to relate to me and to help me?" My response, "For so many years, it has been all about you and getting help for you and your addiction. But this isn't about you. This is about me and getting the help I need to become a more emotionally healthy person." ~Raina

His needs seem to come first. I can't say that prior to a few months ago he had much empathy at least for my needs. ~Ciara

They are married to themselves in every way imaginable. Sex was for him and him alone. His responsibility to the family ended at providing a paycheck after which it was time for a beer and TV. Everything else was my responsibility. ~Trish

How have you experienced the unfaithfulness of your spouse being married to themselves?

He was never devoted to me. ~Alice

Maybe he hasn't technically been "un~Faithful" but then again he hasn't been "faithful." Sure he didn't do the bad of cheating with another woman, but he didn't do the good of supporting and loving me either. He wasn't faithful to love, to protect, to care, to share, to relate. The marital covenant is to be lived out, not just promised once and then not acted upon. He has broken his promise. He has broken the covenant. If a marriage is more than just a physical sexual relationship then why do we rely on that as the only evidence of a marriage promise being broken?? What about the spiritual and emotional intimacy? Do they count for nothing? No, of course not! And that is where he's been unfaithful, in his lack of spiritual and emotional intimacy. ~Wendy

At the same time that he wasn't interested in sex with me, he was often masturbating while looking at porn. ~Raina

I felt aloneness when he was into himself and tripped over himself trying to hide whatever selfish behavior he was enmeshed in. ~Ashley

I have experienced unfaithfulness with his use of porn and masturbation. ~Ciara

His lack of faithfulness was constant. Everything took precedence over me except when I was pregnant. ~Trish

How might you relate to these reasons for staying?

Fear of Being Alone

I didn't want to have to do everything on my own...even though looking back, I did! ~Alice

I feel defective after all these years of not being loved and pursued. I know the Lord loves me and I'm a great treasure in His eyes but this experience does affect me. Who would want me? I'm overweight, I'm damaged goods, I'm used up,

I'm passed over: these thoughts are hard to battle. ~Wendy

This is not an issue—at times I'd rather be alone—it's easier. ~Bev

Fear of Dating Again

I didn't ever want to get into the same nightmare again with another man. ~Alice

There's the fear of not knowing if someone is really who he or she appears to be. The pastor who married us told me that he might be too quiet for me (according to the personality test we took) but I didn't mind that because I knew that he would open up to me eventually. Not true. As a result of my experience with him, I don't know if I can trust a man again, feeling stupid and not knowing if it would be the right one because I was wrong the first time. ~Wendy

I made an active decision some 20 years ago to not allow fear to rule my life. It still permeates from time-to-time; however, I don't fear dating that much because I see it as a form of relating to others. Not that there aren't occasional twinges, but largely I am doing OK. ~Carl

I don't think I would date again. I have too many other things I would want to do with my time, and besides dating is way too complicated at this point! ~Ashley

I can't imagine dating again, how to start, and how to proceed. I don't know if I want to imagine it. ~Ciara

Fear of Impact on my Children

Yes I am fearful. I am a child of divorce and it did definitely

impact me. ~Faith

I wonder how they would handle it, how it would affect their futures? ~Alice

I hate doing this to my kids. I would much rather be in a healthy marriage that lasts for life, but the reality is that I'm not in a healthy marriage, so why would I want it to last for life? The short answer is that I don't. The kids need a father in their lives, but I cannot stay married to him. At this point, it's better we separate or divorce. ~Wendy

This, the potential negative effect of divorce on my kids, has been the main factor in my decision not to divorce my husband. Right now, my husband comes to my parents' house to see my daughter every weekend and I have some control over what they do and don't do. I make sure she eats healthy food and gets to bed mostly on time. However, from conversations my daughter has had with me, I know that she is being impacted just by our separation as she thinks it is unfair her parents aren't together and she says she loves us both and wishes she could live with us both all the time. Her sadness breaks my heart, and so I have given my husband more time to get serious about recovery probably than I should have. Also, I home school our daughter and I have been afraid I would not be able to continue to do that if we divorced as I would need to get a job in order to make more money. ~Raina

They have already been impacted. The impact is definitely there even if my kids can't perceive the effect. ~Ashley

I Don't Want to be Divorced

This is true. I don't want to be divorced after 30 years of struggling to overcome this habitual sin in my marriage. I can't give up now. ~Faith

I did not do anything wrong. I just loved him. Why should I suffer? Why should our kids suffer? ~Alice

I don't want to be divorced. I would prefer that things worked out, but it's beyond my control. It's beyond my influence. I have to accept whatever he chooses. ~Carl

I don't want to be divorced: I truly love her. I love our life we created together and really don't know that this life I love can be recreated with anyone else on the planet. ~Andrew

I never saw myself as being a divorced person. I don't like the idea, but I also don't like staying married in this limbo state. ~Raina

The Money

Definitely a fear and concern. No, money shouldn't be our god, but it does come in handy to live life and raise kids. ~Wendy

I know that money will be much tighter if we divorce. This fact has also played a part in my decision to stay separated and not divorce. However, I have a part-time job that still allows me to home school my daughter and that takes care of some of our financial need. However, I know that my standard of living will have to change if and when we divorce. ~Raina

Like I said before, half of nothing is nothing. By the time I pay lawyers and court fees, sell the house and then divide

what remains in half, there will be nothing. So even if things don't change, if my decision to stay is a logical and honest one, what would be the point in leaving? ~Ashley

The money is nice, but it's not a real deal breaker. ~Bev

Current Lifestyle

I would probably have to go back to work. That would be no big problem as I am educated and skilled though less free time and 1/2 the assets is a painful prospect. ~Faith

We would have to move to a smaller house. ~Alice

Some of my kids will miss living in the country and some will like being closer to things in town. ~Wendy

I would miss his family and our friends. ~Ciara

Nobody Would Understand

Nobody would understand why I would leave my spouse. They see him as easy going, friendly, and just so nice. He has two personalities: the one he shows in public and the one he shows me in private. ~Faith

When I file for divorce, I will be looked at as the bad guy, even though he was un~Faithful to me. If I make it official, I come across as mean and uncaring. I hate being judged. ~Wendy

Because I have a group of strong friends and my core make-up is to be honest and open, I've not had this fear. The more I explain to people, the more I put my story out there, the more that folks (including two counselors) agree that his *choices aren't within my control.* ~Carl

I have friends and family who know about intimacy anorexia, so I think I would be supported. But they, like me, would be sad. ~Andrew

Quite the contrary...I think people would take my side but I would hate for people to hate my husband because in many, many ways, he is an amazing man! ~Ellen

Until I came across the Intimacy Anorexia model as Dr. Weiss describes it, I didn't have a language or a framework to be able to justify divorce to myself, let alone anyone else. Now I have words that would describe the emotional, mental, spiritual and sexual abuse that he has perpetrated. ~Trina

What is Your Reason for Staying

I have hope that he will mature, change, and get help. ~Faith

Fear of what he might do to himself (suicide) and fear that others would blame me for his choice to take his own life. Fear that the kids would later turn on me. ~Alice

I'm waiting for the right time, for example, my son graduating. ~Wendy

I'm not. ~Carl

For some reason, I can't seem to get the guts up to admit to my husband that I want a divorce. There are so many unknowns and a potential resultant change that I guess I am just not ready to face. I know my daughter will be negatively affected by a divorce and that breaks my heart. ~Raina

I feel called to stay. As tough as it is, and sometimes it is really tough, I feel staying is the right thing for me. ~Ashley

I enjoy his companionship and I see progress which gives me hope that our relationship will be more intimate and more fulfilling. ~Ciara

Fear is my reason for staying. Fear won't let me convince myself that I am justified in leaving even when others tell me I am. It just seems wrong for me to leave??! ~Ellen

I see progress. I see what our marriage can be: better than I had originally thought it could ever possibly be. ~Bev

I am staying married to an intimacy anorexic. I don't want to go to the hassle of divorcing and separating all the assets, the house, and the investments. I had already been divorced once before and look how I ended up: In another dead-end marriage. Here I am married to another sexually addicted, intimacy anorexic!!! Now I know how damaging to my heart that the tricks of intimacy anorexia are.

I'm afraid I couldn't make enough money to live and raise the children. ~Trish

Staying? That really is an important question. If you have gotten this far in the book, then you have read and possibly **relived some painful memories. If I haven't seen the miracle** of recovery in my office week after week, year after year, decade after decade, I would give up and tell you to give up.

However, I do see the miracle of men and women heroically defeating their intimacy anorexia and become true lovers and cherishers of their spouse. On the flip side, I have also seen the tragedy of anorexics selfishly clinging to their intimacy anorexia, refusing to change while they continue to inflict pain on their spouses.

In order to correctly judge your spouse's recovery attempts, I want to present the portrait of a hero in recovery. You need this portrait in order to decide whether you should stay with your anorexic spouse based on how closely he or she matches this image of heroism in recovery. Believe behavior. Heroes' behavior although imperfect will look like this:

• They initiate the 3 dailies with you daily (2 feelings, 2 praises and prayer). When they fail to initiate, they must complete their set consequences.

• They initiate sex and are present during sex. If they fail to initiate, they comply with the set consequence.

• They are in intimacy anorexia telephone or local groups.

• They are working through the "Intimacy Anorexia: The Workbook" (Discovery Press, 2010) and "Intimacy Anorexia: The Steps" (Discovery Press, 2010)

• They seek help when they get stuck.

Women and men exhibiting these characteristics make progress such that for the spouse, staying becomes a more attractive option than it was previously. People who, on the other hand, don't exhibit these characteristics are not truly in recovery and are only going to inflict more pain on their spouses.

So, now that you have a picture of what a person staying for looks like, the question becomes this: To stay or not to stay?

The most important thing as you consider staying or not staying is that you are really 100% honest as to why you are choosing to stay. If you are staying for financial reasons, lifestyle, or image then be honest and don't spiritualize or romanticize your true reason. Such romanticizing can only create further dysfunction.

The rest of this chapter is going to be quite a journey. The decision or stay or not stay with the intimacy anorexic spouse and the process that follows is often complex. You will be so tempted to project your own values, your own ability to love and care, onto your spouse. You'll fight your own denial and grief at the prospect of more years of not being loved.

Staying
Option 1

You can stay in the marriage and just accept that this is as good as it gets. Your spouse is probably not going to change or show you any more love than now. His or her anorexia could even worsen progressively making the amount of love you are receiving today from your spouse the most you will ever receive from him or her. However, if you choose this option you must fully accept your spouse the way he or she is right now. You must accept that change may not ever happen. If you don't accept these difficult truths, you will drive the both of you crazy by viewing each new self-help or marriage conference as your savior. You will drive the both of you crazy by constant expectations, constantly disappointed.

When you choose to stay you must accept two other things. First, you must acknowledge and then accept full responsibility for the real reason you stay with your anorexic spouse, whether it be fear of being alone, fear of loss of financial status, maintenance of family image, etc. Secondly, you must grieve your present losses, fully aware that these losses are permanent, fully aware that you have chosen them. Only when you grieve the years or decades of loss can you adapt in your future and build a new life.

Staying with a spouse who is not going to change and might likely even worsen is a real option, a valid option. If this is your choice, stop focusing any energy on changing your spouse and put your energy into adapting your lifestyle and mindset so that you can feasibly live with an intimacy anorexic spouse.

Option 2

Staying and fighting for your marriage is also an option. If you choose this option it is absolutely imperative that you get support for yourself.

Now to be honest, the fact that you're willing to fight for your marriage doesn't mean your spouse is. He or she can still choose anorexia over you. Fighting doesn't guarantee victory for your marriage for victory depends on the both of you.

In fighting you can apply some of the techniques in the Married and Alone Workbook such as the block/punch when the anorexic criticizes, blames, or uses silence or anger. This technique requires that you admit that you feel distant as a result of your spouses' behavior or words. They share with your spouse what he or she can do to nurture you so that you move away from distance.

Another technique you can use is mirroring your spouse's

lack of touch or praise. In some cases this technique is an effective way to show a spouse the pain and damage wrought by his or her behavior.

Getting professional help can help if both are willing to fight for their marriage. Staying and fighting can be tough but I have seen so many marriages saved through this option.

Option 3

This option is to be used only when other options have failed. It involves the use of distance to create pain for the intimacy anorexic spouse based on the principle that addicts often view pain as a motivator for change.

You must realize that not all anorexics value their spouses or their marriages and so some will relish the distance that is a function of this practice. Some will latch on to it and remain there, distant from you, and completely content. For this reason, I just want to warn you: this option doesn't guarantee results because deep down some anorexics do not want to be married at all, thus preferring distance.

Your separating from your spouse can start as simply as sleeping in different rooms in the same house and can progress to a more definite separation. During the time of separation, you and your spouse will both work toward individualized goals. You will both be accountable to a therapist or recovery couple for your progress toward goals. Reconciliation between spouses can start to occur when these goals are met.

Option 4

I was told by a speaker in a seminar that in an ancient society if you murdered someone, even if it is by accident, the dead carcass of your victim would be tied to you. As the dead body decayed, it would begin to eat your body and eventually you would die a horrible death as your sentence.

This is how many spouses feel after fighting for decades for their marriage to someone who doesn't care about the same marriage. They have chosen the cancer of intimacy anorexia by staying with those spouses and are thus slowly and horribly decaying alongside.

If you find yourself at this point, let me share with you a few tips. Some intimacy anorexics are married to the image of marriage (since it makes them appear normal or good), not to you. This type of intimacy anorexic male or female gets really ugly in the divorce process.

So, don't threaten divorce again and again, but you should become informed legally. Know your assets and custody issues. By becoming informed, you can become empowered to make a better decision.

Intimacy anorexics will not file for divorce because divorce would make them look bad. In truth, they could have emotionally divorced you years ago.

I have seen one of the spouses divorce the other because of the anorexic's stubborn refusal to love his or her spouse. The unloved spouse divorces and moves on leading to a much happier life.

Regardless, of what option you choose, you deserve solid information and solid support. You are absolutely worth being loved, even through this process.

Chapter Eleven

Professional Counseling

In addition to the vital attendance and involvement in Twelve Step recovery, many spouses will benefit greatly from professional therapy.

"What? Am I in need of therapy, too?" This very universal response to the suggestion of therapy conjures fear. Does the idea of therapy frighten you? Therapy is nothing to be afraid of; perhaps a general discussion of the types of therapy available might help assuage your fear just as it might help you decide if therapy is for you.

As is true with the fields of medicine or finance, the mental health field is comprised of professionals specializing in a variety of aspects of mental health. These professionals have a wide variety of philosophies and training perspectives, and can meet the different needs spouses of intimacy anorexics have.

Counselors Certified to Treat Sex Addiction (SRTs)

A certified therapist in sexual addiction recovery, or Sexual Recovery Therapist (SRT), trained through the American Association for Sex Addiction Therapists is a Masters level or higher counselor who is licensed by his or her state. This therapist has undergone a minimum of 45 hours of training by Dr. Weiss. He or she has been supervised during their training for a minimum of 6 months by Dr. Weiss or a certified supervisor and has completed a competency exam in sexual addiction.

These counselors are by far the most informed therapists on intimacy anorexia in the counseling field, education about treatment of this condition being a significant component of the SRT's training.

Psychiatrist

Psychiatrists are medical doctors who have attended several years of medical school and are trained to look at biological reasons for problems with the human being. They possess expert knowledge about the medications that influence the chemistry of the brain and thus have the authority to prescribe such medications to patients.

A psychiatrist will most benefit the spouse who might be in need of medication for a condition like depression. Or, if the psychiatrist has had addiction training, or has had exposure to workshops dealing with the effects of intimacy anorexia, he or she may be of help in recovery from the effects of a spouse's intimacy anorexia.

Psychologist

Psychologists and psychiatrists are often confused though they are completely different animals, so to speak. Like psychiatrists, psychologists are doctors though not medical doctors. Their names are preceded by the designations Ph.D. (doctor of philosophy), Ed.D. (doctor of education), or Psy.D. (doctor of psychology). Unlike psychiatrists, psychologists have neither attended nor graduated from medical school. Therefore, they are not licensed physicians and so cannot prescribe medication. They spend their educational training looking at the cognitive aspects of the human, such as IQ, reading and math levels, psychological testing, and the like. They are often trained to do individual, group, and marital therapy.

A psychologist, with a doctorate in psychology, can be of great help to the spouse, especially if the psychologist has had experience working with intimacy anorexics and their spouses. A psychologist can be of help in therapy to a spouse, particularly if the spouse is experiencing a psychological problem, such as depression, suicidal thoughts, or a compulsive eating, sleeping, or alcohol disorder.

Licensed Professional Counselor (LPC)

The Licensed Professional Counselor, or LPC, usually has either master's level training, or Ph.D. level training with expertise in counseling or a field like sociology or anthropology, that focuses on understanding the totality of the human person.

The master's level LPC, much like a psychologist, can be a great resource for a spouses as they deal with their individual problems and with problems affecting their families. An LPC is usually able to identify and deal with issues such as depression, obsessive/compulsive disorders, addictive disorders, co-dependency, etc.

LPC s, like psychiatrists and psychologists, are required to undertake ongoing training and, in most states, will have a **more reasonable fee structures than those of psychiatrists** and psychologists for those seeking counseling. When attempting to choose a Licensed Professional Counselor, first find out how many years prospective counselors have been practicing. Also, review the "Questions to Ask" section at the end of this chapter. These questions along with the **counselor's level of experience will help you to determine** whether the counselor is the right fit for you and for your intimacy anorexic spouse.

Social Workers

Social workers will possess either a bachelor's or a master's degree. They may have several levels of certification which can differ from state to state and may be Certified Social Workers (CSW) or a Masters Level Social Workers (MSSW), depending on their experience. As the title "social worker" **implies, this mental health professional is trained to see is-**sues from a social perspective. Such a perspective is beneficial, **and can be helpful in many cases, but unless the social** worker receives specific training in the field of addictions, **there may be limits as to how helpful this professional can** be for the spouse of the emotional anorexic.

If, however, the family situation necessitates social services for example, finding residential treatment centers, a social worker can be quite a help. Like LPCs, social workers' training and capabilities vary, so when choosing a social worker be sure to find out what exactly each potential social worker's educational training and experience entail. Again, refer to the "Questions to Ask" section at the end of this chapter for further information.

Pastoral Counselors

Pastoral counseling is also available in many areas. Pastoral counselors include people who have professional degrees in counseling from an accredited seminary or religious institution. They may possess a doctoral level education (Ph.D.) or a master's level education, but in many cases—as in the case of many pastors of local congregations—pastoral counselors might be only educated through the bachelor's level. Some may even possess no formal education. We must not be too myopic when looking at educational qualifications though. Pastoral counselors with only small levels of specific mental health education can be still significantly helpful due to strong backgrounds in church settings, complete with cohesive understandings of ~Faith and plenty of experience counseling individuals and couples from a ~Faith perspective. Given the significance of development of spirituality in the recovery of the person, pastoral counselors can be quite helpful.

The strengths of a pastoral counselor would include spiritual training, professional experience, and professional training in the fields of addictions, counseling and/or psychology.

Some possible weaknesses of the pastoral counselor might be a lack of training or skill in some areas deemed necessary by the person seeking treatment and support. For example, the pastor might be well- versed in the travails of the spouse of the intimacy anorexic but may be less well-versed in identifying psychological problems, by virtue of the degree of his training. Pastors are usually not trained counselors, but can be a great support to the spouse of the intimacy anorexic in the recovery process. The pastoral counselor, like all other professionals discussed, should be asked the appropriate questions from the "Questions to Ask" section.

Christian Counseling

Christian counseling is another form of counseling now readily available in larger cities, and more and more in smaller communities. Though in some ways similar to a pastoral counselor, a Christian counselor does not hold a position as a pastor and will not have undergone professional pastoral counselor education training.

A Christian counselor is often professionally trained in the theory of counseling, psychology, and human development. These counselors can be Master's or Doctoral level trained professionals, but as the training that the counselor receives can vary widely, it is wise to check the Christian counselor's training prior to entering into a therapeutic relationship with him or her.

For those who embrace the Christian ~Faith, a Christian counselor presents a definite benefit as this counselor shares the patient's worldview. He or she can integrate biblical truths and biblical understanding into the healing process in a way that will feel comfortable and familiar to the patient. Still, it is once again imperative to ask the questions relating to the training and expertise of these counselors. Just because they are a Christian does not guarantee they understand, or successfully treat, the effects of intimacy anorexia.

Professional Counseling

Certified Alcohol and Drug Addiction Counselors or Licensed Chemical Dependency Counselors

CADACs and LCDCs are available in most areas, although their designations may differ from state to state. These are counselors with a variety of training backgrounds.
Their level of education ranges from a high school diploma to a Ph.D. The counselor's training is always important but is especially important in the case of those who treat addictions. Again, the training of an individual counselor is very significant. This cannot be stressed more than in the field of alcohol and drug addictions. In some states individuals recovering from alcoholism or drug addiction, who want to enter the helping profession, find that such certification is the easiest way into this field. They do have a valid experience and understanding of the addiction process, as well as understanding of the recovery process. However, caution must be used, in that recovering people often have multiple addiction problems. This is something to be noted when interviewing an addictions counselor.

Those interviewing addiction counselors should closely study the prospective counselor's training and experience. In addition, it is important to ask how the counselor may have integrated a Twelve Step philosophy into his or her own life and also how these principles might guide the counselor's practice. Unless a counselor has completed at least a Fourth and Fifth Step and has begun the process of making amends, his or her perceptions might still be clouded by guilt and shame, and the counselor might not be able to facilitate the growth you need in your life.

Strengths of the addiction counselor are many. They are often trained in family systems theory and thus understand family dynamics well. They are familiar with the dynamics of addiction and usually come from a Twelve Step perspective, which, as I have shown, is directly applicable to recovery from the effects of emotional anorexia. Often these counselors have work experience in alcohol and drug addiction treatment centers. Often they share an office with a psychiatrist, psychologist, or master's level counselor and benefit from collaboration with these experts. They are often supervised in their work by a degreed professional. You can find out if a particular counselor's case load is being supervised, and by whom, and what that supervision process is. Finally, in this list of benefits, an addictions counselor would be aware of recovery groups in the area and the importance of support groups.

Marriage and Family Counselors

Like most of the counselors previously discussed, Marriage and Family Counselors can have a variety of educational backgrounds. Marriage and family counselors come from a family systems approach, taking into consideration the needs of the entire family. Because of this perspective, they will be highly attuned to how each family member processes problems, and how the family members interact with each other and will be able to identify any dysfunction that might exist in family dynamics.

Understanding the dysfunction can also help the counselor to suggest opposing helper roles that each family member might naturally fill. For example, the addict is the one who needs help, the wife is the strong one and the chief helper, the children are her supporters, her cheerleaders in helping dad. From a systems approach, a counselor might observe this family and point out the dysfunction inherent in it: in this case, Mom's helper role has squelched her identity, so she needs to once again establish her own identity and boundaries. This way, Mom will not be pigeonholed into one role and, in the case of Dad's recovery, feel purposeless. Highly astute in family dynamics, the marriage and family counselor can be a big help to the spouse of an intimacy anorexic and to the whole family. Refer to the "Questions to Ask" section to determine the training and experience has when seeking this type of counselor.

These questions can help you when selecting the right mental health professional for your needs and the needs of your family. Use them when interviewing prospective counselors.

Questions to Ask

1. Do you have a clear understanding of intimacy anorexia?
2. Do you have experience working with spouses of intimacy anorexics?
3. How many spouses of intimacy anorexics have you counseled in the last two months?
4. Do you have training to do therapy with people with addictions and their families? (State or Board certification)
5. Are you a recovering person working a Twelve Step program?
6. What books have you read on intimacy anorexia and their spouses?
7. Do you have specific training to deal with (if these issues apply to you) rape victims, survivors of child sexual abuse, incest or other trauma?

Telephone Counseling

Because the current number of professionals who successfully treat those affected by intimacy anorexics can be limited-even in the larger metropolitan area, Heart to Heart Counseling Center has established telephone counseling for the spouse of intimacy anorexics, the intimacy anorexic, and for the couple.

Clients using telephone counseling display the same success rate as those who come into the office. This form of counseling is especially helpful for those who travel or work or for those who, given the sensitivity of the subject matter, feel that their confidentiality is of utmost importance. Many physicians, lawyers, ministers, businessmen and students don't want to run into their counselor at the grocery store. In addition, they'd rather not encounter someone they know socially or professionally in the lobby of Heart to Heart's office. For still others, the chief benefit of telephone counseling is the fact that their kids can play quietly in the background during sessions; these clients simply do not have to find a babysitter to watch the children during sessions.

More information can be found at the back of the book on this service.

3 and 5-Day Intensives

Three and Five-Day Intensives sessions are offered out of our offices in Colorado Springs, Colorado. Three sessions are scheduled for couples each day, for three days. This is a great way to get a lot of recovery work done in a very short amount of time. For more information, see our appendix for quotes from previous attendees of our 3 and 5-Day Intensives.

Chapter Twelve

The Twelve Steps

Every spouse of an intimacy anorexic bears scars. Some scars are less severe than others, though, mark my words, all are deeply marred. Just as each survivor's scars are unique, each one's road to recovery, each one's healing process is unique. Still, an almost universally-helpful method aiding in recovery is the twelve step program utilized for the benefit of alcoholics, drug addicts, sex addicts and even workaholics.

In the following pages I will walk you through the principles of the Twelve Steps

The Twelve Steps of Alcoholics Anonymous Adapted for Spouses of Intimacy Anorexics

1. We admitted we were powerless over our spouse's intimacy anorexia--that our lives had become unmanageable.

2. Came to believe that a power greater than ourselves could restore us to sanity.

3. Made a decision to turn our will and our lives over to the care of God as we understood Him.

4. Made a searching and fearless moral inventory of ourselves.

5. Admitted to God, to ourselves, and to another human being the exact nature of our wrongs.

6. Were entirely ready to have God remove all these defects of character.

7. Humbly asked Him to remove our shortcomings.

8. Made a list of all persons we had harmed, and became willing to make amends to them all.

9. Made direct amends to such people wherever possible, except when to do so would injure them or others.

10. Continued to take personal inventory, and when we were wrong, promptly admitted it.

11. Sought through prayer and meditation to improve our conscious contact with God as we understood Him, praying only for knowledge of His will for us and the power to carry that out.

12. Having had a spiritual awakening as the result of these steps, we tried to carry this message to others, and to practice these principles in all our affairs.

Note: The Twelve Steps are reprinted and adapted with

permission of Alcoholics Anonymous World Services, Inc. Permission to reprint and adapt the Twelve Steps does not mean that AA has reviewed or approved the content of this publication, nor that AA agrees with the views expressed herein. AA is a program of recovery from alcoholism. Use of the Twelve Steps in connection with programs and activities which are patterned after AA, but which address other problems, does not imply otherwise.

An Interpretation of the Twelve Steps for Spouses of Intimacy Anorexics

The comments here should not be construed as representing any particular Twelve Step fellowship. They are my own interpretation of the steps from my own experience, as well as from years of clinical experience helping spouses of intimacy anorexics recover through use of the Twelve Step process.

Step One: We admitted we were powerless over our spouse's intimacy anorexia--that our lives had become unmanageable.

We. I am so glad that the first word in the first step is we since I would hate to think a spouse would have to endure this experience alone. Intimacy anorexia is not the problem of an individual but a collective problem, an international problem. "We" means that people can tackle the problem collectively. We means that like it or not, others have been where we have been. We have similarities and similar experiences, most namely   spouses who withhold love and praise. We have experienced being blamed for the distance our spouses created. We is a comforting word in this step because it means we are not—and don't have to be—truly alone. We can heal together, with the help of others like us. We, then, is an essential word. Without each other, we often fail to recover.

Admitted. This is a difficult word. Many times throughout our lives, we have had to admit some wrong doing: Maybe we stole something or hit our little sister and then had to admit what we did. Surely we all remember those feelings of dread directly preceding our admitting to our wrong doing. But despite this dread, we went ahead and admitted it. We told someone what we did and afterward, we felt less burdened. We felt ready to move on. Admitting to the effects of your spouse's intimacy anorexia, and now possibly your own negative issues, is one of the more difficult things we will do in our recovery. Admitting, however, is a very important aspect of your recovery. Only those who admit to something can move forward in recovery and in life.

We Were Powerless. Again, I'm glad that there is a we included here; you are not the only one who is powerless. Moving on to the idea of power and its opposite, power is often used as a synonym from control. He who holds power can have control over others. So powerlessness, then, denotes a loss of control, a tough reality for every spouse of an intimacy anorexic. Our powerlessness moves us toward others though, toward a group of like-minded people. Here we can admit our powerlessness. We have tried to change our spouses. We have failed.

Spouse's Intimacy Anorexia. Being powerless over our spouses' intimacy anorexia is difficult. Often the attempts to be more for them so that they will love us have failed. Our attempts to love them more so we will experience their love in return have likewise failed. We thought if we loved them enough, we could change them. This belief, sadly, is an erroneous one.
The fact remains that your spouse is an intimacy anorexic.

She or he was an intimacy anorexic before you met and may be one in the future as well. If you didn't cause this condition, you can't cure it. When we accept this truth, we assert our powerlessness over our spouse's intimacy anorexia.

That Our Lives. Our lives are the very core of us, our identities. Life is the inner part of us that identifies us as being separate from others. Our lives have been affected by our spouses' intimacy anorexia.

Had Become. These two words indicate to me that our feeling of powerlessness has been developing slowly. It has taken time for us to find ourselves in our current state. It didn't just happen overnight though: our powerlessness was shaped by our own choices and the choices of our spouses.

Unmanageable. When we think about manageability, we think about things being in order, about serenity. Manageability, then, makes us think of disorganization and chaos. It makes us think "What a mess!" Sometimes this is the way we feel, and our feelings can be valid. Our lives, in many of the areas we have talked about, have become unmanageable, unconnected, uncontrollable, and unpredictable. No matter how hard we have tried to make our lives look good or perfect, they are not. Now through Step One, if we can admit this unmanageability, we have a strong hope of recovery.

I encourage everyone to take Step One seriously, because it is the foundation of the Twelve Step program. It will build you a good house of recovery to live in in the future.

For further in depth step work on Step One and all of the Twelve Steps for spouses, I encourage you to use the workbook Married and Alone: The Twelve Step Guide. This guide is specifically for spouses of intimacy anorexics. This is made available through Heart to Heart Counseling Center. You will find ordering directions are in the back of this book.

Step Two: Came to believe that a power greater than ourselves could restore us to sanity.

Came to Believe. Again notice the step is written in the past tense. The original steps were written to share the process that the original members of AA went through in recovery. There was a process through which they came to believe.

It is really a simple process. You come to believe many things during your lifetime. For example, you came to believe that there was a Santa Claus. Later you came to believe that there wasn't a Santa Claus. As you grew older, you may have come to believe that a certain person liked you, and later realized they didn't like you. You come to believe certain religious and political dogmas and ideologies. In each of these processes there is a definite point at which you understood or came to believe.

In Twelve Step groups, the process of coming to believe is something that often happens as a result of exposure to other recovering people. You may not necessarily know the date, or the hour, when you did come to believe, but you know that you did feel differently, and you began to have hope. This "a-ha" moment is so important in recovery, because knowing that you have come to believe, or knowing you do believe can save your life. This coming to believe can save you from the hopelessness and feelings of guilt and worthlessness that many spouses of intimacy anorexics experience. If you have come to believe, you can have hope in God help or maybe hope that you did not cause your spouse's intimacy anorexia. You can heal regardless of your spouse's choice to stay anorexic.

A Power. A is a common word. You use it every day. A cat, a dog, a book--and in every context in which it is used, it denotes one. If you were going to use a word to describe more than one, you would say "these," or another word that indicates plurality. This step is not written in the plural. This power is "a" power, a single power greater than ourselves. The singularity denoted by "a" is significant. It indicates one entity, one strength, one energy, one spirit, one power. When you come to believe, you are believing in one being.

Greater Than Ourselves. You now realize that there is one that is greater than ourselves. This is the best news you have in recovery: that you don't have to solve this fearsome puzzle alone but can rely on the one power. As you begin to trust this power, you begin to recover from the sick patterns, poor choices, and undesirable relationship patterns that have been so much a part of your marriage.

In the original context of AA, this power greater than ourselves indicated that the power was greater than that first group of recovering alcoholics. This one single power was greater than a whole group. That's a lot of power. People in recovery frequently first recognize this power in the group, but in reality it is greater than the group. Even if you had a power greater than yourself, you may have had difficulty accessing the resources of that power and applying them to your life. In the program, you come to believe that this power has more ability to solve life's problems than you do alone. What a relief!

Could. Could is one of the most helpful, loving expressions in the Twelve Steps. Could this power have the ability, the resources, the energy, the intention of helping you along in the recovery process? The implied answer is yes. It is possible now to begin to be restored. It is possible now to begin to be healthy, to have loving relationships with loving people, to be loved and nurtured in a healthy way. It can be done, and this power working through us can do it. It is the experience of many spouses in recovery that, if given the freedom and the opportunity, if you quit trying to do it all on your own, this power will do for you what you have been unable, or unwilling to do for yourself. All you have to do is ask.

Restore Us to Sanity. **Restore means bringing something back.** Frequently when you think of restoration, you think of an individual tinkering on an automobile or repainting an old house, eventually making both look like new. The same is true for those recovering from the effects of their spouses' intimacy anorexia.

Spouses have for so long been robbed of intimacy, trust, and even a strong sense of their own reality. In a world that should have been safe, these spouses were violated again and again.

And a sort of insanity can be the result of this violation. It can be a natural result of living with a condition as bewildering as intimacy anorexia. You may not consider yourself insane, and clinically speaking, you're not, but living in two realities at the same time, and living with a secret, can make most spouses feel insane. You try again and again to do something that should work, but it doesn't. You try, and try, to fix the problems that intimacy anorexia creates in your life, without success.

The fact that you continue to try to fix your spouse, fix your life, never stopping to realize that your methods are not working, qualifies you as one who need to be restored to sanity. For, as they say, doing the same thing while expecting different results is just plain crazy. Never fear though! It is possible for spouses of intimacy anorexia to be restored to sanity. This restoration is real: Those already in recovery have experienced it. They are living proof that it is possible to make better choices, and they are living proof that you, reader, can also be restored. You may still feel crazy, but if you have gotten this far in your recovery, you have a good chance of finding sanity.

Step Three: Made a decision to turn our wills and our lives over to the care of God, as we understood Him.

Made. Similarly to the word "became," made" indicates a process involving time and choices, and like all processes, a completion point can and should always be reached. For example, when kids in school construct an ashtray, or a meal or dress in home economics, or a table in shop, there is a time for the process and a time for completion, the step when the dress or table is finished, made.

Made is something that has been coming along, but is finally resolved to the point that you can say it is done.

A. Here again we come to that little word a. Indicating it is one, one moment, one event. Many people want to spread this step out, but it cannot be so. This step must be cloaked in finality. We only make this decision one time, but we make it with surety.

Decision. When making a decision, people often list the good and the bad, the pros and cons, associated with a situation. The same is true for Step Three.

Using a marital analogy, while Step Two is similar to an engagement period, Step Three is the marriage ceremony itself. To explain, Step Two involves getting to know: you get to know your power is greater than yourself, and you began to get comfortable with the idea of having God in your life. During Step Three you make a commitment to share your life with God. This decision to commit is a one-time event, but it provides a means for further growth.

To Turn. Someone once said that to turn means to flip over, kind of like a hot cake is flipped on a griddle when one side is done.

This hotcake analogy defines "turn" pretty simply but also pretty profoundly. If you flip over, you make a total change from the way you have been up to this point.

Highways all over the world indicate directions for turning: signs may indicate a left or right turn, or U-turn. What you do in Step Three is definitely a U-turn as, in committing to Step Three, you turn away from your limited understanding of how life should be. You leave behind perceptions, experiences, and ideas about things you thought you understood. In turning from them, you gain a completely new perspective. This shift in perspective is an essential part of recovery. You are turning, becoming, and it is amazing how far that turn can take you, as you continue in your movement toward recovery.

Our Wills. Again, the plurality of this wording indicates that the group stays and works together. In this group of safe people who have turned their wills and lives over to God you will begin to see the decision to make a break from the emotional anorexic as a possibility for yourself. But what is your will? The simplest definition of will is probably the ability to make choices. In the group you will begin to turn over the choices that you make to God. You must turn your choices over to God, try to understand God's perspective, and let that perspective be a lens through which you view your decisions and your life. Step Three is so powerful because of this life-altering aspect.

Many recovery groups use the phrase "stinking thinking" which refers to a dysfunctional thought patterns that inhabit the minds of addicts, or in this case anorexics or spouses of anorexics. Stinking thinking is the faulty way that a burdened, unrecovered person thinks. This thinking doesn't work. The choices of unrecovered people make don't bring about positive results. There seems to be certain self-destructiveness to their choices and behavior. Step Three cuts to the core of stinking thinking and helps individuals to throw off destructive patterns thus enabling them to begin new lifestyles.

Dedicating our wills and our thoughts—which drive our wills—to God creates a dynamic of true safety. When making decisions about relationships, we are now able to turn to God for help. As we do, God will demonstrate new directions we can take, and new choices we can make; we will begin to find freedom. We will begin getting answers, and will be able to make different choices about our relationships. This is a freedom that is only gained by submitting our wills to God, sharing the responsibility of choosing with God.

Our Lives. Our lives come to be as they are as the result of all of our choices be they spiritual, physical, emotional, financial, social or sexual. When you turn over all of these aspects, you give yourself to God. You begin to trust God and in trusting God, you begin to believe that God will take care of you.

You may say: "This is frightening. How can I trust God?!" Respond to your own very natural question by simply looking at what you have trusted in the past. At—arguably—your best, you have trusted your own ability to think, your own ability to make choices. At your worst, you have taken the advice of a few chosen people who have not acted in your best interests.

Turning your will and life over to God is necessary, for God will always act in man's best interest. It is through this experiment of trying to trust God that you will see that God is trustworthy. Only when you take the risk to need God and He can reach out in love in response to that need. Only then can you begin to believe that God loves you. And through realizing the truth about God's love, you begin once again to trust yourself. Eventually, you can even regain your trust in people. Step Three is an essential part of working the steps. It is not a luxury. It is necessary for a healthy, happy life. Working the steps is not always easy, and often you do not understand why you must work them. Often the steps are understood only after they have been completed. Then you realize the beauty of this spiritual process, and open yourself to further growth and joy, as you walk this road with others who are making the same steps toward recovery.

The Care of God. Human demonstrations of kindness, commitment, patience, nurturing, and acceptance are all demonstrations of care.   Does God's care comprise some of the same behaviors? Yes, God's care is God's willingness to be involved in a nurturing, supportive, accepting way, in your life. God is in a very real way concerned for all; God is concerned for the spouses of intimacy anorexics. You can sometimes see God's care more clearly in the lives of others than you can in your own life. For this reason, support groups can be helpful, especially for the spouses of intimacy anorexics. The group can be easily perceived as a manifestation of the care of God in their lives, both as a collective representation of God's supportive nature and as a treasure trove of examples of God's power to transform. It is possible for you, by looking at others in your support group, to connect with individuals—thus seeing their own pain and seeing their own slow but eventual triumph over that pain—in such a way that it radically changes your life. Something as simple as their support can be seen as the extension of God's care and concern.

Now, we'll talk about God. The original writers of the Twelve Steps changed only one word from their initial version. In Step Two they changed the word "God" to "a Power greater than ourselves." That is the only change they made, and it was made for this reason: those first alcoholics said that God was too scary for the recovering person in Step Two. Maybe the recovering person had too many hurts, too many problems with God, so the word was changed to "a Power greater than ourselves" to give the newcomer an engagement period, and allow him or her to experience God through the group's care, nurturing, and love. In this way they could come to believe in a caring God who could and would help them.

But, let me back up to a more foundational concept: who is God? Let me share my thoughts with you on this subject. Simply put, God is Love. God is also omnipotent, all-powerful, in authority or in control, a great helper for those who turn their lives and will over to Him, and who give God the authority they have previously claimed as their own.

According to what you have learned so far in the steps, God has the ability to restore you. God is more powerful than you are alone, or in a group. God is one who gets actively involved in your life, one who has more power, and more success, than you in dealing with the effects of intimacy anorexia. This God can and will help you as you work the Twelve Steps.

For many this understanding of God will develop into a faith that is common in the American culture, and will enable the recovering spouse to enjoy the benefits of finding a community that shares the same faith. Some will not. It is a universal blessing of this program, however that they can, if they are willing, come to a greater relationship with God, as they understand God.

Those who have turned their wills and lives over to the care of a God they understand, who have turned their choices over to God, often have more understanding of how God works, and how God thinks. The group is a good resource, especially for those early in recovery who want an understanding of God. It is very important to realize, as it pertains to understanding God, that no single person is going to understand the totality of God, but the members of your support group can be helpful in this journey.

As We Understood God. Our understanding of God hinges upon our understanding of the nature of "relationship," since to understand God is to be in relationship with Him. When you first meet someone, your knowledge of him or her is limited. Only through time, communication, and commitment, do you really come to understand another person. The same is true in your relationship with God: It requires the same time, commitment, and communication. In addition, as previously stated, this relationship with God requires a willingness to surrender our wills to God. And in surrendering our wills, our minds can be transformed into minds that seek good, leading to a new freedom and happiness, in short, a new life. This is the beauty of finding God in the Twelve Steps.

Step Four: Made a searching and fearless moral inventory of ourselves.

Made A Searching. When you search, you intend to find something. For example, when you lose your keys, you go searching with the intent of finding the keys. As you begin your inventory, you are searching, scrutinizing, seeking with intent, to find something significant that might bring you relief.

In this context, searching indicates that you will have to expend some energy. This is the beginning of what is often referred to in the program as the "action steps." You now begin to take action on your own behalf. Note that this step is also in the past tense. As you begin your inventory, you can know that others have passed this way before, have survived, and have gotten better. You are not alone.

Fearless. Fearless simply means without fear. This is the best attitude with which to approach your moral inventory. Being fearless allows you to view your inventory objectively, even when you become immersed in the pain that you will inevitably uncover as you look at ways you have been wounded.

Your fearlessness might aid you in facing a childhood wound or it may aid you in facing the reality of your spousal relationship and, in many cases, facing the role you might have played in building the relationship's negative dynamic.

Moral. **Something moral exudes virtue. It is upright. Something immoral stinks of vice and violation of conscience.** As
you look at your life in Step Four, you will be looking for
things which you've done which have violated your conscience. As a very basic example, we can all relate to the
case of the child stealing the cookie from the cookie jar. The
child had been warned to leave the cookie jar alone and so,
to the child, touching the contents of the jar has become
wrong. Still, the desire for cookies remains strong in the
child such that when the parent's back is turned, the child
snatches and devours the cookie. Immediately, though, he
feels remorse for his action has violated his conscience.

In Step Four, you will also be looking at how you were violated by others. Have you ever said to yourself, "If they
really knew me, they wouldn't like me. If they knew I was
sexually abused or that my spouse is an intimacy anorexic,
they wouldn't be my friend." The shame and guilt you carry,
from the actions of other people toward you, can be overwhelming. **Step Four is designed to release you from that
shame and guilt** as you look at how your moral code has
been violated by others.

It is wrong to believe that you are unworthy because of your
past. In recovery, you come to know yourself and let others
know you. Step Four is about coming to know yourself, being honest with yourself about what happened, taking into
account how it affected your life, and where it leaves you
today. In short, Step Four is an inventory. You will list everything that happened, even if it involved others and you
were simply an innocent bystander, as in the case of the divorce of a parent. Such an event may not have had anything
to do with your morality, but it did affect you emotionally.

Inventory. What are you to inventory in Step Four? You inventory your experiences. You inventory your memory. Many see this inventory as a life story. It is a process where you begin to see the truth of what you've done, and what has been done to you. Just as a merchant inventories both items he values and items he wants to rid himself of, you will categorize both the negative and the positive. And like the merchant—who keeps meticulous records, you will write down your inventory.

Because of the written nature of this inventory, you will need to have the necessary materials on hand: pen or pencil, paper, and a quiet place where you can be uninterrupted. There is no right or wrong way to write an inventory. Some just begin writing. Some organize their inventory by ages and then begin filling in events that fit into certain spans of time, such as birth-to six years, six to twelve years, and so on. Still others have first listed all the traumatic events they can remember--things that were done to them, or by them, that violated their value system, then writing how they felt at the time, and how they feel now about those events. The most important quality of the inventory is that you do it.

Take courage though. You will be face to face, for perhaps the first time, with the total reality of your life. It can be pretty overwhelming, so don't be afraid to let your sponsor or therapist know how you are feeling while writing your inventory. As you transfer your story to paper, you are also transferring the pain, guilt and shame onto paper. Though the experience of facing your pain and shame can be traumatic temporarily, writing an inventory can be a very positive, transforming experience in the long term, and it is vital to your recovery from the effects of your spouse's intimacy anorexia.

Of Ourselves. **Once again, you can see this is a plural** denotation. Just as others have survived the pain of record- ing their inventories, you will survive. **Just as others have been freed from their shame, you will be freed.** And despite the plurality just discussed, you must be reminded that only you can do this for yourself. Only you know your pain, the strength of your fears, your deepest secrets. **Only you are** qualified to write this inventory, to remember who you have been, to accept who you are, and to decide who you want to be. There is great freedom in taking your focus off what is wrong with others, and doing a searching and fearless mor- al inventory of yourself. **You may not understand the value** of this step until you have completed it, but it is well worth the pain and tears.

Step Five: Admitted to God, to ourselves, and to another hu- man being the exact nature of our wrongs.

Admitted. **Here you are again, looking at that word admit-** ted. You already know that it means to fess up, or acknowl- edge, what is true. **All of us already experienced the pain** and joy of admitting something, probably as a child or ado- lescent. **Do you remember your feelings of guilt and shame,** like you had let yourself and others down? And how, despite these guilty feelings, you somehow summoned the courage to admit what you had done. You admitted the truth--no matter the consequences. And this admission transformed your feelings: now you felt better. The secret is out.

The same is true in Step Five. You admit all that you have **confessed in your Fourth Step. You let out all those secrets** and finally let in that clean joy which comes from truly being totally known.

To God. God might be the easiest person to tell. Or He might be the hardest, depending on your relationship with Him. If you feel God has historically been one who will only let you down, admitting what has been wrong in your life can be particularly difficult because God is not someone you trust. Fortunately God is indeed trustworthy. And beyond that, He is generous, forgiving of all the wrong that you have done and is willing to restore any and all of your broken- ness. As one wise person in recovery stated, "It's okay to tell God. God already knows it all anyway and is just waiting for us to be honest about it, too."

To Ourselves. If you have been truly fearless and thorough when recording the sins of your past, you will have admit- ted several things to yourself. You will have admitted your powerlessness. You will have admitted your profound amazement at your poor choices, your sincere sense of hav- ing failed yourself, and your need to be restored to sanity. Acknowledging the truth about what you have done is prob- ably the most humbling experience you will have.

It is at this point though, that your recovery of your true self is finally possible for in acknowledging the past, you can let it go and move forward, toward a new future. You are now able to begin a more shame-free life. This ability will empower you to experience the next, and most essential, part of Step Five: being able to reveal yourself to another human being.

And to Another Human Being. "What? I have to tell all this stuff to somebody else? I have to look that person in the eye and admit all of the wrong I have done?" The answer to these questions, quite simply, is "yes." Telling your story to another human being is the most crucial part of your recov- ery. In writing your Fourth Step, you have poured out into one place your total history of shame, hurt, abandonment, abuse, acting-out, and poor choices. Cataloguing such a vast amount of negativity has likely dredged up a great amount of pain. If all this pain is kept inside you, and is not shared with another human being, the pain may propel to you, once again, convincing yourself that you are unworthy of love because your past. You could use the totality of your negative past history, self-condemnation, instead for healing. In order to prevent ourselves turning inward, we must turn outward, to others, or in this case, to one other person. In unburdening ourselves to another person, you will likely experience catharsis, a lightening of our load.

Coupled with this catharsis borne of unburdening is the reassurance by a trusted friend that nothing you have done makes you unlovable. Now someone knows the whole truth, and still loves you. What a remarkable feeling!

A note of caution is appropriate here: When you choose someone to hear your Fifth Step, it is important to pick someone you trust, someone who will listen without condemnation, someone who will understand that you are digging into your past, in order to make your present and future better.

The Exact Nature of Our Wrongs. The fact that this part of the step is so specific will help two kinds of people: those who say, "I can't be specific, so I'll never really feel loved," and those who believe that they can own everybody else's wrongs, and avoid looking at their own choices. The first person needs to be specific in sharing their story, because the shame they experience about the past is not to shame them for their past. This can be a memory tied to specific episodes. We must talk about those specific episodes to relieve the shame associated with them. The second person needs to acknowledge their own shortcomings and "clean their own side of the street," not anyone else's, so that they too, can be freed from their own shame.

It's a recognized fact that you can't free anyone else from their shame. Each person has to work their own program of recovery, in order to have the kind of happy and fulfilling life we are all capable of experiencing.

Step Six: Were entirely ready to have God remove all these defects of character.

Were Entirely Ready. Now, because you have acknowledged your powerlessness, catalogued the truth about your past, admitted your past to someone, all the while seeking the God of your understanding, you are ready. You have completed the core of the first five steps, learning to "trust God and clean house."

Now you must learn how to maintain the cleanliness of your house--preventative maintenance.

You start by remembering that you are entirely ready. You are 100 percent ready to see the trash for what it is, and to refuse to let said trash once again build up in your house. You might be quite attached to some of this trash. You hesitate to give it up, telling yourself that it might come in handy some day. Being entirely ready, though, means that you are ready to see the trash as negative material. You are ready to banish it from your life, for good.

You finally realize that changing is not quite as frightening as staying the same.

To Have God. Having God in our lives is so significant for spouses of intimacy anorexics. Here, in Step Six, they are reminded that they, like all who seek a relationship with God, are blessed to have one. They are beginning to believe that God does want the best for them, that God is willing to work with them in their continued efforts to move toward recovery.

Remove All. This step may sound painful and those in recovery might wonder how this removal will take place. It is not up to you to decide how removal will take place; it's only up to you to be ready. Remember that earlier you recognized that you don't have a whole lot of power of your own. In Step Six you will rely on God to have the power to perform this removal in order to transform you.

Defects of Character. Review your inventory for an illustration of your character defects. One common defect you might detect is negative ways of expressing anger. Another is the tendency to try to control loved ones. Honesty is important in listing these and other defects. By acknowledging and then allowing these defects to be rooted out recovering spouses become more healthy and honest themselves; thus, they gravitate toward more healthy, honest people. Understanding this can certainly motivate you to really look at your defects of character, and be 100 percent willing to have God remove them. This is the real release that prevents the dust and trash from resettling in your house.

Step Seven: Humbly asked God to remove our shortcomings.

Humbly. Many struggle with the word humble, having been humiliated, time and again, by the spouses of intimacy anorexia. Humility though is not the same as humiliation. Humility, in this case, means recognizing your true humanity. Humility means knowing that you don't have the power to change yourself. Only God does.

Asked God. Humility requires that we ask, not tell, God to heal us. You are asking, in a sense, to do God's will.

To Remove Our Shortcomings. **God will be with you through-out your life, removing your shortcomings as you continue to identify them when they surface, as long as you are will-ing to ask for help.**

You can trust that if you ask, God will remove your defects of character, no matter how much you resist. If you decide to hold on to these defects, you will be fighting a losing battle. If you choose this losing battle, you will really need your support group to acknowledge that you are holding on **where you should let go. They will also give you support** as you try new behaviors, in place of the old ones that kept **you so unhappy. Allow them to support you in this growth process.**

Step Eight: Made a list of all persons we had harmed, and became willing to make amends to them all.

Made A List. **You probably don't have any problem shop-ping for groceries if you've made a list. You know that the** most efficient way to shop is using a written list. The same is true for your list of those you have hurt. Take a pencil and **paper in hand, and, reviewing your inventory once again,** make a list of the names of all those you have harmed. This list should include yourself, and can also include what dam-age was done.

Of All Persons. **Be honest.**

We Had Harmed. Previously, you have looked at how you have been harmed. But that is only half of the story and you can only be halfway healed. Now, it's time to take on the other half.

And Became Willing. The past tense here reminds you, one more time, that the hard work demanded in the previous steps is survivable. Spouses have worked their way through these steps before, and have found peace and happiness on the other side. It also indicates a process. Recovery doesn't just happen overnight. Becoming willing takes time for everyone, especially if they are holding on to a victim status.

To Make Amends. Making amends means acknowledging the wrong you have done, and being willing to be different. You stop blaming other people in order to justify your own behavior. You stop rationalizing, and you stop avoiding responsibility.

To Them All. No stone should be left unturned at this point, or you will still carry old guilt that will keep you stuck in old sick patterns of thinking and relating. With names, phone numbers, and accounts of damages in hand, you are ready to move on.

Step Nine: Made direct amends to such people wherever possible, except when to do so would injure them or others.

Made Direct Amends. In Step Eight, you made your list. Now you go to the people on your list in order to make direct amends to them for the inappropriate attitudes or behaviors you have had in the past.

Be honest with yourself as you ask each person on your list for their forgiveness. When you acknowledge your wrong-doing, you will find incredible freedom. Tremendous emotional weights can be lifted; often relationships can be restored. This is not a 100 percent guarantee, since some relationships will remain fractured. However, at least your side of the street will be clean.

It is not a given that the other person will ask forgiveness in return, even though they may have injured you much more than you have injured them. Your goal is to clean your own slate. You are not responsible for what others leave undone, nor can their shortcomings keep you from recovering and feeling good about yourself.

Except When To Do So Would Injure Them or Others. You may become confused when you attempt to decide if making amends will injure the person involved, or be detrimental to other, possibly innocent, people. Such confusion is best resolved with the assistance of a group, sponsor, or therapist. Confusion is not to be used, however, as an excuse to shirk the responsibility of making amends.

What you must consider when admitting past behavior is whether or not your confession would so significantly damage the other person involved that you should not raise the issue to them. You can ask yourself, "Would this be damaging?" If you have a question, do not assume you have the answer. You could very possibly avoid an amend which could restore a relationship, or hold on to an amend that will set you up for old behavior. Go over your list with a sponsor, support group, or therapist, if at all possible.

Step Ten: Continued to take personal inventory and when we were wrong, promptly admitted it.

Continued. Here again you must deal with the maintenance of your newly clean house. You are not letting the dust fall. You are not letting the dirt collect, or the garbage flow over the edge of the garbage can. Today, when you have been inappropriate or have violated anyone's boundaries, including your own, you don't have to wait five or ten years to make amends. You can make amends now and keep making amends as needed as you go along.

To Take Personal Inventory. Taking a daily personal inventory is a process in which spouses are able to look at each person in their lives, and see how they are interacting with these people. They look at their attitudes toward others and honestly evaluate them.

And When We Were Wrong, Promptly Admitted It. You will be wrong, sometimes many times in one day. When you are wrong, promptly admit it. Promptness is necessary because it keeps you from holding on to the baggage, thinking for far too long about whether you were or weren't wrong. Promptly means admit it right now, right here. If you have been acting inappropriately, say, "I'm sorry. Forgive me, I'm acting inappropriately." It is as simple as that. This step gives you a way to stay free from the bondage of guilt and shame. It keeps you humble, which often helps you to remain healthy.

Step Eleven: Sought through prayer and meditation to improve our conscious contact with God as we understood Him, praying only for knowledge of His will for us and the power to carry that out.

Sought Through Prayer and Meditation. You are seeking. You are looking to improve your relationship with God using the spiritual means of prayer and meditation. Prayer is verbal, and often verbal-turned-inward communication with God. Prayer is a way of seeking God. In the past, you may have put very little effort into finding God, and when life took a negative turn, you felt abandoned by God, despite your lack of relationship with Him, a lack directly attributable to your lack of effort. It has been said many times in meetings, "If you can't find God, guess who moved?" You move away from God. God never moves away from you. Seeking Him is all that it takes to find Him.

Meditation is a sometimes deeper sense of prayer. Prayer is requesting, asking, interacting. Meditation is listening and hearing God's voice. Many experience rest and peace through meditation and are able to still the constant obsessive thinking that prevents them from hearing what God has to say: that they are significant, they are loved, and they deserve to be healthy. Meditate on God's character, on your personal relationship with Him, on some scripture or recovery material you have, and allow the truth of your belovedness to really sink in to your spirit. Be still, and God will speak to you.

To Improve Our Conscious Contact With God. Step Eleven reminds you to keep God in your conscious mind rather than ignoring God most of the time, only turning to Him when you have thoroughly botched your life. Keeping God at the forefront of your thoughts will enable you to experience God's power and love of God in a whole new way. Therefore, you will experience life in a whole new way. You will have a higher sense of purpose and greater joy. In short, you will have a better relationship with God.

As We Understood God. It is impossible for any one of us to totally understand God. Indeed, my understanding of God might not work for you, nor yours for me. The beauty of the program is that you can begin to see evidence of God, in other people. You won't come to a new understanding of God on your own; instead, you will do so as you interact with the people in your support group, church, and community. As you listen to and observe others as they talk about their experiences with God, you will grow in your own understanding.

Praying Only For Knowledge of God's Will For Us. By now you are beginning to see the benefits of letting go of self will. In Step Eleven, you are gently reminded that when you pray for God's will in your life; in doing so, you are asking for the absolute best solution to whatever problem you are facing. The realization that you can trust God to show you the best solutions is a positive one, a life-changing one. The people, places, and things you have given your will over to in the past did not always—or even often—have your best interests at heart. You realize this, and because you now trust God you can say, "Not my will, but thy will be done."

And The Power to Carry That Out. You pray for knowledge of God's will, not just for the sake of having the information, but also for the power to carry it out. After all, what is the point of having information if we possess no forward momentum leading us toward acting upon this information. Sometimes, in a response to your prayer for knowledge and for motivation, a path will become clear. Often the power, to make the changes God seems to want you to make, comes as a result of the encouragement of the people in your support groups. This power can also come through your observation of an individual stuck in old behaviors. Your motivation to change can come from seeing the consequences others are experiencing because of their unwillingness to act differently. Once having asked for direction and listened for guidance, you can act with assurance, knowing that you are likely on the right track, knowing that if by chance you are on the wrong one, you will come to know it.

Step Twelve: Having had a spiritual awakening as the result of these steps, we tried to carry this message to others and to practice these principles in all our affairs.

Having Had A Spiritual Awakening As The Result Of These Steps. It is no wonder that an individual who comes to the steps, and in the process of time admits to powerlessness, the frailty of being human, the need for a relationship with God, actively pursues that relationship, cleans house, makes amends, and maintains this behavior. This individual, then, unsurprisingly, has a spiritual awakening. This spiritual awakening has been the goal all along, the purpose for the working of steps one through eleven. And what a worthy goal this awakening is! Here the spouse discovers he has worth and value, that he has been loved all along by God, and that he can be loved by others, if he will only believe in his "lovableness" and open up his heart so that love can come in. He can now come to see himself as a precious child of a loving God. This awareness changes everything and in particular changes the way he will be able to treat himself, and accordingly, others.

We Tried to Carry This Message to Others. In the beginning of Alcoholics Anonymous, it was not a matter of a drunk alcoholic seeking advice and support from someone who was sober. It was the recovering alcoholic who sought out the active drinker. After seeking this advice, Bill W, the cofounder of AA, knew that if he couldn't share what advice he had received, what he had discovered about his relationship with God and its importance to his sobriety, he wouldn't be able to stay sober. The same principal applies to spouses of intimacy anorexics: they need the messages that only survivors of intimacy anorexia can provide. In the same way, spouses of intimacy anorexics need to share their stories. And as they progress in their recovery and become less absorbed in their own pain, they will begin to be able to turn their gaze outward, to see opportunities to share their experiences, and their resultant hope with other spouses who are suffering from the same low self-esteem, and boundary problems that you experienced. And they will share for no other reason but that they remain mindful of the miracle of recovery they have been privileged to experience. Constant reminders of this miracle are necessary because without constant reminders, they are likely to forget where their strength and health have come from. Forgetting can, then, easily lead to complacency.

One of the truest sayings around recovery groups is, "You can't keep it, if you don't give it away." The door to recovery was only open to you in the first place, because others passed through it before you did. Therefore, it is your joy and your responsibility, to keep the door open for those who follow after you. This is the only way to ensure freedom for all.

And To Practice These Principles In All Our Affairs. Here is the most practical part of the Twelve Steps: Take what you have learned and keep doing it every day. Like the athlete who must exercise daily to stay in shape, you need to practice daily the new skills you have learned, so you can stay in good emotional and spiritual shape. Practice admitting your powerlessness over the problems in your life. Practice acknowledging God's superior ability to run your life. Practice avoiding old behaviors. Practice new thinking and behavior skills. Practice prayer and meditation.

Just as you ended up with low self-esteem and an utter lack of boundaries after many years practicing destructive behaviors, becoming the new, emotionally healthy person you want to be will take practice.

Congratulations to all who have found the courage to embark on this journey of the Twelve Steps. These steps, when followed, are a tried and true path toward healing from the effects of being in a relationship with an intimacy anorexic. You may not have caused the pain you experience, but you are the one now responsible to heal your pain from your spouse's anorexia; you are the only one who can do so. The spouses I have counseled, that are most successful in this healing process, are those who actively worked the Twelve Steps.

Appendix

Feelings List

1. I feel (put word here) when (put a present situation when you feel this).
2. I first remember feeling (put the same feeling word here) when (explain earliest occurrence of this feeling).
Rules For Couples: 1- No examples about each other or the relationship. 2-Eye contact. 3-No feedback

Abandoned	Aware	Close	Deprived	Feisty
Abused	Awestruck	Cold	Deserted	Ferocious
Aching	Badgered	Comfortable	Desirable	Foolish
Accepted	Baited	Comforted	Desired	Forced
Accused	Bashful	Competent	Despair	Forceful
Accepting	Battered	Competitive	Despondent	Forgiven
Admired	Beaten	Complacent	Destroyed	Forgotten
Adored	Beautiful	Complete	Different	Free
Adventurous	Belligerent	Confident	Dirty	Friendly
Affectionate	Belittled	Confused	Disenchanted	Frightened
Agony	Bereaved	Considerate	Disgusted	Frustrated
Alienated	Betrayed	Consumed	Disinterested	Full
Aloof	Bewildered	Content	Dispirited	Funny
Aggravated	Blamed	Cool	Distressed	Furious
Agreeable	Blaming	Courageous	Distrustful	Gay
Aggressive	Bonded	Courteous	Distrusted	Generous
Alive	Bored	Coy	Disturbed	Grouchy
Alone	Bothered	Crabby	Dominated	Grumpy
Alluring	Brave	Cranky	Domineering	Hard
Amazed	Breathless	Crazy	Doomed	Harried
Amused	Bristling	Creative	Doubtful	Hassled
Angry	Broken-up	Critical	Dreadful	Healthy
Anguished	Bruised	Criticized	Eager	Helpful
Annoyed	Bubbly	Cross	Ecstatic	Helpless
Anxious	Burdened	Crushed	Edgy	Hesitant
Apart	Burned	Cuddly	Edified	High
Apathetic	Callous	Curious	Elated	Hollow
Apologetic	Calm	Cut	Embarrassed	Honest
Appreciated	Capable	Damned	Empowered	Hopeful
Appreciative	Captivated	Dangerous	Empty	Hopeless
Apprehensive	Carefree	Daring	Enraged	Horrified
Appropriate	Careful	Dead	Enraptured	Hostile
Approved	Careless	Deceived	Enthusiastic	Humiliated
Argumentative	Caring	Deceptive	Enticed	Hurried
Aroused	Cautious	Defensive	Esteemed	Hurt
Astonished	Certain	Delicate	Exasperated	Hyper
Assertive	Chased	Delighted	Excited	Ignorant
Attached	Cheated	Demeaned	Exhilarated	Joyous
Attacked	Cheerful	Demoralized	Exposed	Lively
Attentive	Childlike	Dependent	Fake	Lonely
Attractive	Choked Up	Depressed	Fascinated	Loose

Lost	Pretty	Separated	Ticked	Weak
Loving	Proud	Sensuous	Tickled	Whipped
Low	Pulled apart	Sexy	Tight	Whole
Lucky	Put down	Shattered	Timid	Wicked
Lustful	Puzzled	Shocked	Tired	Wild
Mad	Quarrelsome	Shot down	Tolerant	Willing
Maudlin	Queer	Shy	Tormented	Wiped out
Malicious	Quiet	Sickened	Torn	Wishful
Mean	Raped	Silly	Tortured	Withdrawn
Miserable	Ravished	Sincere	Touched	Wonderful
Misunder-	Ravishing	Sinking	Trapped	Worried
stood	Real	Smart	Tremendous	Worthy
Moody	Refreshed	Smothered	Tricked	
Morose	Regretful	Smug	Trusted	
Mournful	Rejected	Sneaky	Trustful	
Mystified	Rejuvenated	Snowed	Trusting	
Nasty	Rejecting	Soft	Ugly	
Nervous	Relaxed	Solid	Unacceptable	
Nice	Relieved	Solitary	Unapproachable	
Numb	Remarkable	Sorry	Unaware	
Nurtured	Remembered	Spacey	Uncertain	
Nuts	Removed	Special	Uncomfortable	
Obsessed	Repulsed	Spiteful	Under control	
Offended	Repulsive	Spontaneous	Understanding	
Open	Resentful	Squelched	Understood	
Ornery	Resistant	Starved	Undesirable	
Out of	Responsible	Stiff	Unfriendly	
control	Responsive	Stimulated	Ungrateful	
Overcome	Repressed	Stifled	Unified	
Overjoyed	Respected	Strangled	Unhappy	
Overpowered	Restless	Strong	Unimpressed	
Overwhelmed	Revolved	Stubborn	Unsafe	
Pampered	Riled	Stuck	Unstable	
Panicked	Rotten	Stunned	Upset	
Paralyzed	Ruined	Stupid	Uptight	
Paranoid	Sad	Subdued	Used	
Patient	Safe	Submissive	Useful	
Peaceful	Satiated	Successful	Useless	
Pensive	Satisfied	Suffocated	Unworthy	
Perceptive	Scared	Sure	Validated	
Perturbed	Scolded	Sweet	Valuable	
Phony	Scorned	Sympathy	Valued	
Pleasant	Scrutinized	Tainted	Victorious	
Pleased	Secure	Tearful	Violated	
Positive	Seduced	Tender	Violent	
Powerless	Seductive	Tense	Voluptuous	
Present	Self-centered	Terrific	Vulnerable	
Precious	Self-conscious	Terrified	Warm	
Pressured	Selfish	Thrilled	Wary	

Guideline #1:
No Examples about Each Other

Guideline #2:
Maintain Eye Contact

Guideline #3:
No Feedback

Sexual Recovery Materials

Intimacy Anorexia Materials

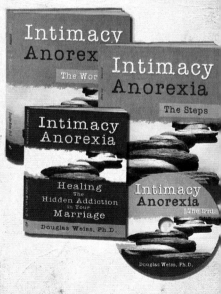

719.278.3708

Additional Recovery Resources

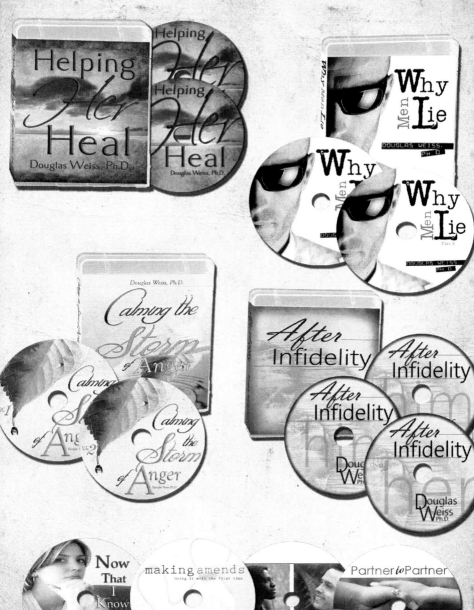

Marriage Materials

Youth/Singles Materials

719.278.3708

Conferences with Dr. Weiss

- Men
- Marriage
- Women
- Youth

Visit us at:
www.drdougweiss.org

Take men on a journey through these clean principles. The DVD and Workbook will allow some greatcoversations. You can change men's lives forever aand be part of the solution for men in your church or community.

719.278.3708

Dr. Weiss has created a 45-hour program to train counselors how t work with sexual addicts and partners of sexual addicts. Th DVD/Workbook training set is available for anyone who would like t have more information on treating sexual addiction. Everyone who com pletes this 45-hour course will receive a certificate of completion. Th course is for anyone who has a significant interest in the field of sexu addiction. This course can be taken by anyone who wants to increas their knowledge of sex addiction and partner's recovery.

This course is also part of certifying licensed counselors to become cer tified as a Sexual Recovery Therapist (SRT). If you or a counselor yo know has an interest in treating sexual addicts or their spouses call th phone number below.

For more information
or to place an order,
please call:

719.330.2425

or visit us at:

www.aasat.org